"The first time I went to [ ] [Lib-]erty Bell fell on my head," Howard Rosenman, a Los Angeles-based film producer, told *Vanity Fair*. "Here was this gorgeous Jewish chick who obviously came from a sophisticated, neurotic Texas Jewish background, talking in the [language] of my generation, bringing together strands of sociology, politics, anthropology, history, science, and the Bible. The community she's addressing is a group that partied and drugged and sexualized through the sixties and seventies, and here comes this woman who looks like one of us, who you know could have been at Studio 54 or dancing at Fire Island Pines with a tambourine on her hip—and yet she's talking like Jesus Christ. She's talking about the most fundamental precepts. She's talking about the Golden Rule."

Marianne WILLIAMSON

HER LIFE
HER MESSAGE
HER MIRACLES

ELENA OUMANO

ST. MARTIN'S PAPERBACKS

MARIANNE WILLIAMSON: HER LIFE, HER MESSAGE, HER MIRACLES

Copyright © 1992 by Elena Oumano.

Cover photograph by Berry Berenson, Perkins/Sygma.

ISBN: 0-312-95041-1

Printed in the United States of America

St. Martin's Paperbacks edition/November 1992

10 9 8 7 6 5 4 3 2

For my brothers, Robert and Lawrence Shamis

ACKNOWLEDGMENTS

I want to thank the many people who helped me with this book. Special thanks to my agent, Madeleine Morel of 2M Communications, for her hard work, creativity, and faith in me, to my editor, Charles Spicer, for his patience and support, and also to Karen and Rich Clayton, Gina Cuomo-VanPatten, Bob Cook, Eugene Pascal, Nathan Jackson, Jib Fowles, and Farin Greer, for reasons they will understand. I would also like to thank Marianne Williamson's friends and associates for their insightful comments and invaluable help in researching this manuscript.

TABLE OF CONTENTS

CHAPTER ONE

INTRODUCTION

On October 6, 1991, Elizabeth Taylor married for the eighth time in a ceremony at Michael Jackson's ranch in the small town of Santa Ynez, near Santa Barbara. Marianne Williamson was the officiating minister; along with the stars who had arrived by limo and helicopter to witness the event of the decade, she, too, had to dodge press and paparazzi.

At forty years old, Marianne Williamson is being touted as the high priestess of the New Age, the most visible spokesperson of *A Course in Miracles*. A 1200-page, three volume self-study program in "spiritual psychotherapy," the course teaches how to relinquish a thought system based on fear and separation and replace it with one grounded in unity and love.

At the time of the Taylor-Fortensky nuptials, up to five thousand people from Los Angeles to New York were crowding rented halls and churches weekly to hear her standing-room-only inspirational lectures.

Slim, beautiful, and stylishly outfitted in designer fashions, Williamson's blend of thirty-something cynicism with a Pollyana's insistence on viewing the world through the eyes of love has proved to be a winning formula. With hilarious wit, compassion, and unadulterated horse sense, she has taken such honeyed New Ageisms as hope and a joyous perspective out of the closet and made them plausible, hip, propositions, even for the most jaded.

"She's the Joan Rivers of the spiritual world," says Mimi O'Connor, Williamson's former personal assistant.

During a Williamson lecture at Manhattan's Town Hall, *The New York Times* reported, a man asked a question that would unnerve the average guru but failed to ruffle a single Williamson feather. How does the course address masturbation, he wanted to know, since "the course tells us that the purpose of our bodies is communication."

"Interesting question," Williamson shot back, with the lightning sting of a stand-up comic dispensing with a heckler. "In fact, I had one masturbation question in L.A. very similar to this, and I said to the woman, 'Are you from New York?'"

To another woman whose childhood spent in a "psychospiritual cult" had given her a bad attitude about meditation, Marianne advised, "Go meditate. Charles Manson ate apples. That doesn't mean I'm not going to."

Williamson's audience encompasses a broad spectrum of today's talk-show-savvy population and serious spiritual seekers—the addicted and their enablers, the gay and the straight, the young and the old, the affluent and the wannabes. In other words, anyone who feels victimized and/or estranged by an increasingly Kafkaesque society. Sprinkled among the ordinary folk in her audience are Hollywood's biggest players and luminaries, such as David Geffen, Barry Diller, Cher, Shirley MacLaine, Roseanna Arquette, Roy Scheider, and Anthony Perkins. Williamson has been spotted lunching with Hollywood executive Dawn Steele, actress and former roommate Laura Dern. More publicity-shy celebrities, such as Barbra Streisand, gobble up Marianne's sage wisdom via audiotapes of her lectures, with such titles as "Happiness Is a Decision," "Fear of Intimacy," "Obsessive Relationships," "Romantic Addictions," "Try a Little Tenderness," "Ultimate Escape: Blaming Others," and "The Commitment to Serve."

"I thought she was the most brilliant extemporaneous speaker I had ever seen," says Gary Donzig, executive producer of *Murphy Brown,* who attended his first Williamson lecture four years ago. "Originally I thought she must be working off something she had written, but after a period of time I became aware that, no, she was just running with whatever idea she decided to speak on for the day. That was what impressed me most. Her understanding of this complex material and the way she could apply it, using incidents from her own life, was amazing. Her humor was astonishing to me, and she exuded an enormous amount of warmth and charm. I'm afraid to use the word 'charismatic,' but she was charismatic. She was not a charismatic, but she was charismatic."

By the time of the Taylor-Fortensky nuptials, Williamson's charities, the Center for Living, in New York and Los Angeles, and Los Angeles's Project Angel Food, had grown in a few short years from tiny grassroots organizations, staffed by volunteers drawn from her lecture audience, to providing nonmedical support to thousands faced with the challenge of AIDS and other life-threatening illness. Many who had attended her lectures had been inspired to found their own philanthropic endeavors.

Williamson's clear-eyed spin on such issues as intimacy, relationships, money, careers, and the world situation, as well as her abundant good works, had magnetized high-profile support, endorsements, and over a million dollars in donations for her charities from the likes of Geffen, Diller, Bette Midler, Kevin Costner, Kim Basinger, Richard Gere, Harrison Ford, Whoopi Goldberg, David Hockney, Elton John, and David Lynch.

In February 1992, Williamson appeared on *Oprah Winfrey* to promote her first book, *A Return to Love* (HarperCollins), based on *A Course in Miracles* and the themes of her lectures. "I have never been as moved by a book as I have by Marianne Williamson's *A Return to Love,*" Winfrey declared to twenty million television viewers. "I want to tell you all that since I read this book, I have experienced—I've stopped counting—at least one hundred fifty-seven miracles." After proclaiming that Williamson "saved my life," Winfrey passed out one thousand copies of the book to her studio audience. To meet the sudden demand, HarperCollins hastily flooded bookstores with copies of the book. *Return* leapt to number one on the best-seller lists on the very day of its official publication, where it remained for nineteen weeks, and Norman Lear threw a party to launch Williamson's promotional tour.

Nine years earlier, Marianne had left her hometown of Houston, her mom's Oldsmobile packed with a few possessions and the three-volume *Course in Miracles,* a rudderless young woman searching for meaning and direction. Today, like it or not, she has become a major celebrity. But Williamson does not live in grand celeb style. Until she finally bought a house in the summer of 1992, she and her two-year-old daughter occupied a modest two-bedroom West Hollywood condominium, and she made her way around town in a battered 1983 black Peugeot.

For the past nine years, this single mom has kept to a grueling—even impossible—schedule, filled with acts of service to others. She lectured three or four times a week and ran weekly support groups in Los Angeles, lectured and ran another support group once a month in New York, served as president of the board for both the Los Angeles and New York Center for Living, officiated at countless funerals and weddings, visited the ill and dying at their bedsides at all hours of the day or night, and gave individual counseling sessions to whomever asked —often offering her own money along with advice and prayer. "She has an uncanny way of listening to someone and getting an instant gestalt understand-

ing of whatever the situation is," says Ellie Ellsworth, who organizes Williamson's lectures in New
York City. "She can say one or two things and it's as
if you've been stung. It's the awakening of some information inside of you. Every time I would have a
conversation with her, things would start to move in
my life."

Williamson's breakneck schedule merely expanded further when, on May 21, 1990, she became
the delighted mother of India Emmaline, whose father she refuses to name. And in early 1992, after
her book's publication, Williamson managed to
squeeze in a whirlwind national book tour, during
which she autographed copies of her book, lectured,
and appeared on radio and television shows and at
various public events.

"What I need is a vacation," Williamson recently
told a reporter. And though it seems she may finally
prune her overgrown schedule, in actuality she has
merely transfered her humanitarian service to a
wider sphere. Though she continues to support her
charities in spirit and through huge donations from
her book royalties, in spring of 1992 Williamson
stepped down as president of the board for the Los
Angeles Center for Living, and afterward took her
first respite from her rigorous lecture schedule to
begin work on her next two books.

Although others have lectured on the course, and
Jerry Jampowlski's best-seller, *Love is Letting Go of
Fear*, based on some course principles, enjoyed
great success, no interpreter of *A Course in Miracles*
has touched such a powerful, elemental chord.

As of this writing, *A Return to Love* has sold 750,000 copies in hard print. Audiotapes of the book have sold 35,000 copies. Even *A Course in Miracles* shows signs of an increase in sales and has become one of the top ten best-sellers on the religious list of *Publisher's Weekly*.

Although it remains to be seen whether or not *A Return to Love* will lead to a significant growth in the numbers who actually study *A Course in Miracles*, it is clear that as Williamson's profile soars, the message of the course is being delivered to millions.

Williamson has made unconditional love, nonjudgment, and forgiveness—concepts that sound wonderful in theory but are maddeningly elusive to put into practice—reasonable and plausible goals. In fact, when she speaks, they seem a necessary balm to heal this wounded planet.

In *Grand Canyon,* the latest film to feature a group of alienated baby boomers, Danny Glover's character speaks to the postwar generation's hurt and confusion: "Man, the world ain't supposed to work like this. I mean, maybe you don't know that, but this ain't the way it's supposed to be. . . . Everything's supposed to be different than what it is."

The landscape of the nineties and the future that looms before us is pocked with grave problems and the threat of disaster. Says Sandy Gallin, a producer/manager and Williamson supporter, "Put together the ecological breakdown, disease and recession: we gotta pray to get out of this one." Williamson teaches people disillusioned with formal religious systems how to pray and to hope again. In

the age of AIDS, she has lightened the weight of re-
crimination and judgment with compassion and acceptance, and she has literally helped thousands of
people to die with dignity and peace. For a society
increasingly disconnected and unbuttressed by
traditional family structures, she provides a sense
of community. In a time of widespread unemploy-
ment, poverty, escalating civil unrest, drug use, vio-
lent crime, and imminent ecological calamity,
Williamson offers the only true miracle, a shift in
our perception of ourselves, each other, and the
world, from fear to love. "The basic premise of *A
Course in Miracles* is that it teaches us to relinquish
thoughts based on fear and to accept instead
thoughts based on love," says Williamson. "That
shift in thinking brings about a radical transformation and healing. The only way to do that is to re-
move the obstacles in your thinking that prevent
you from approaching all aspects of your life with
love."

Since *A Course in Miracles* was first published in
1976, it has sold over 800,000 copies and spawned
more than one thousand study groups in the United
States and abroad. The people in these groups ex-
amine their spiritual lives and relationships according to the insights and daily lessons that were
"scribed" or dictated to an atheistic, Jewish, New
York psychologist named Helen Schucman. A nag-
ging inner voice, which later was revealed to be that
of Jesus Christ, repeatedly told the harried woman,
"This is a course in miracles. Please take notes," until at last Schucman did—beginning in 1965 and

continuing for seven arduous years. Though full of Freudian and Christic terminology, the course redefines that language and contradicts traditional Christianity on many points, offering instead a corrective to the errors in interpretation of Jesus' original message. Some course practitioners elect to become course teachers; some who practice course principles continue to attend other religious services. But there is no organization, hierarchy, or leadership—only the Foundation for Inner Peace, which publishes books and oversees its translations into other languages. Says Russell Chandler, who wrote a book on New Age groups, "What began as an obscure manuscript has been quietly transformed into a teaching phenomenon."

"Only love is real," Williamson asserts over and over again to her audiences and readers. "Nothing else exists."

Southern California, Williamson's adopted home, has a long and checkered history with mystic revealers. Los Angeles in particular has been characterized in the popular media as a palm-tree-dotted, smog-choked, last-ditch community of star-struck hopefuls, the end-of-the-line stop for American's wanderers, dreamers, and failures, whose hopeful westward passage has been stymied by the wall of the Pacific Ocean. Even if they have achieved success, the rest of the country would sniff that it's only the most superficial kind. These "losers," popular wisdom says, are willing to chance just about anything to redeem their failed pasts. Southern California is fertile field for those who promise to reveal the metaphysical secrets of the universe—everyone from Aimee Semple McPherson to Krishnamurti. Yet if Armageddon can be headed off from anywhere, it's from this sprawling community of the gloriously eccentric and the just plain addled, where space is still made for true visionaries such as Marianne Williamson to be heard. And if the success of *A Return to Love* is any barometer, California dreaming is spreading across our troubled country. Williamson herself says that inspirational speakers "are to the nineties what musicians were to the sixties." If so, she is riding high at the top of the charts.

Hers is the voice heard most clearly above the din of New Age babble. "The course gets through in its way, but I can hear the way she phrases something," says a follower. "The way she speaks about life's situations comes up like the hook of a song sometimes. Her phrasing and especially her humor are two of her great tools. She can get through a thick wall with that humor and break down someone's resistance. You can't help but laugh, and you get the information at the same time."

Aside from Williamson's considerable charisma and her application of a wealth of knowledge, what sets her apart from the rest of the tenders to the spirit are two qualities. One, "to love" for Williamson is not merely a condition of being but an action:

> Spiritual seeking without service is self-indulgent. People who are into crystals and rainbows and who use spiritual principles as a how-to to help you get what you want—

that's not what *A Course in Miracles* is about.

It's a course in *miracles,* not a course in moving furniture. *A Course in Miracles* is about serious devotion to the idea that you are healed to the extent that you allow your life to be used. Service is a direct beam to God. Cynicism is easy; anyone can sneer and jeer. Hope is born of participating in hopeful solutions. As we said in the Sixties, if you're not part of the solution, you're part of the problem.

Secondly, unlike virtually every other spiritual leader in search of a flock, Williamson refuses to ascend the pedestal normally assigned to spiritual leaders. She consistently defines her role as spiritual companion. "What makes it so real for me," says a course student, "is that she will talk in her lectures about her own failings or 'I try so hard to live up to what the course says and sometimes I want to throw the book across the room.' She talks about how she falls short, and you think, 'My God, she is such an expert, and if she can fall short, then it's okay that I do. There's hope for me.' We're all on the path and nobody has it down. I don't know any enlightened masters walking around."

This controversial single mom from Houston, Texas—dubbed by one observer as "an est trainer who found God"—has managed to create a bridge between the marijuana-hazed rebellious idealism of the sixties and a compassionate, *grown-up* actualization of those earlier impulses. Williamson is, in effect, offering a sound program to heal troubled souls and, to use the currently fashionable parlance, our dysfunctional society. Her appeal for social action is the next logical step, the missing link, and the perfect antidote to the disastrous effects of the rampant narcissism and greed that ruled the eighties. Her refusal to play "Great Mother" to her minions is the perfect prescription, rebounding the responsibility for growth and change right back where it belongs, in our own hands.

"The subject tonight is intimacy. I bet you think it's everybody else's problem," she told a Town Hall audience that had braved freezing New York City winter winds to wait in line for her lecture. When the laughter subsided, she offered a course perspective on the latest pop-psych wisdom. "If Mother Teresa were in this country, people would be saying, 'Is that woman an enabler or what!' We'll accept it in Mother Teresa because she's old and in India, but here we talk about codependency all the time," she said. "It's our excuse for being cold and selfish. Nurturing one another is what it's all about, and this generation has a long way to go before we love too much."

"There was a wonderful confluence," says a Hollywood film producer, "of what Marianne had to say and what the community needed to hear."

"Marianne speaks for us," says another course follower. "She speaks in our time, our age, with our specific neurosis, with our particular culture, our particular worldview, and we can relate to the way she speaks about things because she speaks for a great group of us who are hip but are scared, who are into the life and reasonably successful but need help. She speaks for us, and she's one of us. She *is* us. And she has the wisdom every once in a while when we forget, 'Oh yeah, you mean I should wear the pretty nightie; he might come over tonight?' 'Oh you mean I should love myself first?'"

Williamson insists her personal appeal is not the point, that she is no guru, only a fellow student "giving a book report," but she has clearly captured the spirit of the moment in spectacular fashion. And that can have dangerous consequences. It seems to be the fate of those who achieve the stature of public icon to receive along with the accolades and adulation whatever dark shadows we refuse to confront in our own natures and prefer to project onto these larger-than-life luminaries.

"Hollywood's ticket to God," "Guru of the moment," "Mother Teresa of the nineties," "A prophet for the New Age," are some of the labels pinned on Williamson in major profiles that have appeared in *Vanity Fair, People, Time, Newsweek,* and the German magazine *Stern,* to name only a few. Williamson chafes against the inflation of those tags, knowing full well that the pendulum must swing in the polar direction, knocking the idol off the pedestal and flat on its face.

But we seem to feel better when we are prostrate before an object of worship, and even better when we can find an excuse to point to its feet of clay. So despite her incessant disclaimers and protests, for many in her audience Williamson became such an object.

Reverend Sandy Scott, herself an influential figure in Southern California's New Age circles, comments that "Care-givers are a deadly group. Marianne has the care-giver mentality serving her. They serve out of their pain, and the minute you are not an angel, they're wounded."

So as the influence of this self-described "non-denominational minister/priest/lecturer/teacher" grew and her ties to Hollywood's movers and shakers were publicized, so did tensions within the organizations of the Center for Living in Los Angeles and New York, and with the explosions that detonated on both coasts came the inevitable backlash criticism and the betrayals, magnified and distorted by some of the print media for public consumption.

Accusations of financial impropriety were impossible. Williamson had never taken a dime in payment for her work with any of her charities; in fact, she had often dipped into her own pocket to help them through lean times. The critical articles that appeared early in 1992, in *People* magazine and the *Los Angeles Times,* focused on infighting and changes of directorship within the centers, and featured quotes from mostly anonymous sources charging Williamson with subverting her own causes with hypocrisy, self-promotion, an overweaning lust for control, and an ungovernable temper.

Williamson had always acknowledged openly her human imperfections to her audience, presenting herself as a representative fellow student struggling with the same personal issues we all do.

"Marianne is not some stone statue in a church," says Pat Buckley, a psychotherapist based in New York City and a course follower, "but someone on the same journey and process we all are. Being spiritual does *not* mean you never get upset or angry or anything else humans do. It does not mean you must be 'perfect.' If we believed we were 'perfect,' we would not need this classroom called 'the world.' Being spiritual simply means someone is seeking their truth."

"She allows herself to be a leader with clay feet as she's talking to you, says Jodie Elliot, a University of Houston professor who came to study the course through her son. "What that does, ironically, is build your belief in her authority because the position that she describes herself in when she found the course is so completely different from the person we see now. We know that she accepted principles that were positive, and her life has been changed because of it."

Richard Cooper, Williamson's best friend and one of several godparents to her daughter Emma, wonders if Williamson hasn't empowered some people excessively. "If you empower the other person too much their ego can take over. All of a sudden, they think they're the whole show and they forget what she did for them," he says. "I know she gave some people not only their careers, but money! She'd say to people 'I love you so much, you're so incredible,' and they became 'so incredible' that they dropped her. I've seen it happen over and over.

"Some of the things that people fault her on are her greatest strengths," Cooper notes. "This is a true original, and a true original throws people. She's a spiritual teacher. If you want to be close to her, whether you work with her or you're a friend, you will be confronted with yourself. Because she can't do what she does in the world and not have it affect her so deeply. I've never seen someone so spiritual be so daring, to show what's going on. If she's angry, she's angry. She doesn't pretend to be Madam Syrupy. She'll be who she is where she is. I've learned so much about self-expression and about saying what's so from being around Marianne. Sometimes it pushes your buttons, but it's been such a gift to me. I'm allowed to say what I need to say. Always. And I give her the same gift. But I've never seen her not do her spiritual homework. She will hold the goal for forgiveness; she will hold the goal for peace. If you are *A Course in Miracles* student, as you advance, you learn that this is about the peeling of the psyche. She's never claimed to be an enlightened master. Yet her lessons are more intense, perhaps, than those of others, because it's a constant cleansing, and she always holds to it."

"I'm a normal human being just like everybody else, going through my own problems," she insists. "I don't claim to be a saint. I work on my issues like everyone. I try to be a good woman. The course is very antiguru. It very specifically points you back to yourself and your own inner experience as the source of wisdom and decision making. It's very big on personal responsibility, and states clearly that we're equally all teachers and all students."

Stuart Altschuler was the first executive director for the Los Angeles Center for Living. When he was fired by Williamson after a year, he was initially hurt and bitter. His relationship with Williamson has healed, and he now heads his own organization, The International Center for Better Health. His perspective on Williamson's work remains sound. "What I've been taught by Marianne, Louise Hayes, Sally Fisher, Sandy Scott, Sondra Ray, and all the spiritual trainers, is that the way to open your heart is through service. Marianne is a prime example of what it means to be of service on the planet. The Center for Living and her lectures are about being of service. Everything she touches and does is her attempt to serve the planet and humanity. Once I got that, I realized I'd always known that's what I'm here for. To me, that's greatness, and I've always had a sense I was here for a bigger purpose than to sit in the fear. I was always deathly afraid to talk in front of people, to let anybody know who I was. I can speak anywhere about anything now, with very little advance preparation, and it really is about getting out of my own way and knowing that whatever I talk about is about God, spirit, and service. Again, that's something else I learned from Marianne's demonstration. There are so many people in this town who are doing the same thing and who came out of those lectures and started all sorts of service projects."

Williamson remains baffled by the controversy surrounding her. She is simply doing what she loves, undergoing the same growth processes everyone else goes through, hoping to deepen her ability to practice the course principles she preaches. While she jokes about the pitfalls of celebrity—one Halloween she arrived for her lecture dressed like an angel and announced that "I wanted to be Tammy Fay Baker, but they wouldn't let me!"—the distorted public portrayals and the undermining of her position, at the Los Angeles Center for Living in particular, have caused her grievous pain.

"The central theme of the course in terms of the ego system is special relationships," says Kenneth Wapnick, author of several books on *A Course in Miracles*, head of the Foundation for *A Course in Miracles*, and a close friend and associate of the two people whose joining together was the immediate stimulus for the scribing of the course.

Specialness comes in two forms: special hate, directed to people whom we overtly hate and attack, and special love, directed to those people whom we really hate but we think we love. These are the people we put up on pedestals, but as the course explains, underneath all special love is hate. If I put you up on a pedestal, I think you're the wisest, most beautiful, most handsome person in the whole world. That means that I'm not all those things because one of the keynotes of the ego system is if *you* have something, then *I* don't have it. If you have all of this, then that means God loves you and doesn't love me. If He doesn't love me and He loves you, my ego tells me, the reason is because you stole that love from me. In other words, I put you up on a pedestal, but secretly my ego tells me everything you have you took from me. Therefore, I am justified in taking it back from you. I lie in wait until I find a fault in you. When I find that fault, I seize on it and I kill you.

That's what the course refers to as the Laws of Chaos, which is a very important section in the text. That's the insanity upon which everything rests in the world. So any-time anyone puts you up on a pedestal, you know they secretly hate you and that at some point that hate will break through and the love will disappear. Every therapist un-derstands that mechanism. What the world calls love is really hate parading as love. Or, "I need something from you, but I have to pay you for it. I have to make some kind of bargain with you so you'll give me the love, attention, and affection I want but don't be-lieve I deserve. So I have to put on a beauti-ful face, seem to be something I'm not, and then offer you something." That's the kind of special relationship bargain.

That's the part of the course that's most difficult. That's the part most people don't want to look at because it's where the real guilt and pain are. Basically that's where Jesus describes what the world did with Him. In effect, it made Him into a special love object which everyone ended up hating. That's why people ended up killing people in His name. It makes no sense.

As a diligent student of the course, Williamson is familiar with the quirky psychology of special relationships. She also knows what happens—both within oneself and from outside—when one commits to a spiritual path. "A lot of people think if they give their life to God, everything is going to be hunky-dory," she says. "But if you give your life to God, everything that could piss you off is on its way. Of course, everything that is a threat to you is going to come up so that you can work through it. Everything that you could learn is going to present itself."

The myth of Prometheus, known as the Great Cosmic Social Worker, provides a poetic, even lurid illustration of the savagery that can fuel resistance to enlightenment. A half human, half god known as a titan, Prometheus is a key archetype in the New Age movement because he dared to steal fire (that is, consciousness) from the gods. Our desire to reach for the heavens in order to become more conscious belongs to the realm of Prometheus. He is gifted with foresight, and he also differs from other mortals because the goddess Athena has taught him architecture, astronomy, mathematics, medicine, metallurgy—all the arts and sciences. Prometheus' cultural impulse lifts him above the crude and instinctual. He is the first man. As such, he becomes an ambassador of selfless goodwill, wishing only to raise other mortals above their base animal origins. This Promethean urge toward ascension is central to *A Course in Miracles* and to Marianne Williamson's life purpose.

As the daughter of a respected activist/immigration lawyer, Williamson seeks to advance her legacy. "Social revolution is at the center of my being," she told *Vanity Fair*, "but ultimately I had to realize that love is a more revolutionary position than hatred as a motivator; it's less sensational but more effective. My interest is in the creation of an enlightened society."

In the myth of Prometheus, the titan complains constantly to Zeus and other Olympians that man should be endowed with these godlike qualities. Zeus, however, is a tyrannical ruler who does not take kindly toward Prometheus' request. Prometheus presses more and more to allow man to develop toward civility and consciousness, and Zeus becomes increasingly furious. Prometheus, in turn, barely hides his contempt for the jealous god. He eventually tricks and humiliates Zeus, for which he's sorely punished.

Prometheus suffers various forms of revenge at Zeus' hand, the most emblematic of which is being chained to a rock where a vulture feeds nightly from his liver. Hercules finally pleads successfully for Prometheus' release. Prometheus is allowed to live, but because he was initially condemned to everlasting punishment, Zeus stipulates that he must continue to appear to be a prisoner by wearing a ring. In honor of their benefactor, mankind began wearing rings and using wreaths.

According to the seminal psychoanalyst and philosopher Carl Gunther Jung, the drama represented by Prometheus—stealing from the gods and risking their wrath—is a metaphor for the human impulse to "steal" from our own unconscious, that is, the part of our deepest knowing that bridges our corporeal and divine aspects. The Promethean impulse is that which tries to link those aspects, in effect "robbing" the gods and making consciousness human.

Prometheus redeemed mankind from darkness, but even more important, he represents the spiritual urge, the ascensionist impulse away from what is undeveloped, and for doing this, he had to be punished. Zeus' rage and Prometheus' torture represent the reactionary drive in the opposite direction, toward unconsciousness. Whether that punishment is self-inflicted because of one's hidden fears of spiritual awakening, or inflicted upon Promethean characters such as Marianne Williamson by the unconscious segment of society, this split between the urge to consciousness and the drive to unconsciousness is one we all confront.

Williamson could take a page from Judith Skutch, the first person who lectured on the course. Copublisher of the course with her ex-husband, Bob Skutch, and overseer of its translation into other languages, in the late seventies and early eighties she traveled the country speaking on *A Course in Miracles.* "Marianne is just a person doing a job," says Skutch. "She's out there saying what she really believes. She never said she's perfect. My eighty-five-year-old mother says to me sometimes when I carry on about something, 'Honey, why are you so upset? I thought you were a student of the *Course in Miracles*.' And I'll say, 'Yes! I'm a *student*!' "

"I'm deeply grateful to have been allowed to perform this particular service," Skutch says of her lecturing days. "But I needed to turn away from the public role; I realized that it was eating me up. Once, after a very intense week at a college where I was speaking three times a day and conducting workshops in between, someone literally picked up the hem of a long dress I was wearing and kissed it. Whether it was a gesture of just plain love or there was a humorous twinkle in her eye, that was the day I decided, 'I don't want to do this anymore.' "

Monday, June 1, 1992, seven P.M., a balmy late spring evening in the Southern California beach community of Santa Monica. After nine years of never once disappointing her audience, Marianne Williamson is about to deliver her last regularly scheduled lecture. Across the street from the broad stretch of Pacific coastline, the Starlight Ballroom of the Sheraton Miramar Hotel is filling up with her faithful, come for a last fix, as well as a surprising number of those who are grabbing their last chance to hear Williamson speak. The tables set up in the back and at the sides of the hall are doing a brisk business in Project Angel Food T-shirts (though Marianne no longer has formal ties to the organization), copies of *A Course in Miracles* and *A Return to Love*, and cassette tapes of previous lectures. The folding chairs in the front rows are already claimed. The air is charged with an urgent excitement. To-night, it is rumored, Marianne will be talking about *herself*, possibly even addressing accusations made about her in the press.

At seven-thirty on the dot, Marianne strides to the podium dressed in a fashionable aqua fitted jacket that matches her short, slim skirt and spike heels. Her sleekly cut, shoulder-length dark hair frames a strong jaw, porcelain complexion, and large, intense brown eyes. But Williamson's been upstaged. All eyes are on the dark-eyed blond cherub she carries in her arms. Surrounded by a sea of applauding, oohing and aahing adults, India Emmaline Williamson remains uncharacteristically and resolutely sol-emn-faced and silent. "Say hi! Wave! How old are you?" her mother urges gently, then smiles and gives in: "Say good-bye." She passes her daughter to a handsome man who takes Emma in his arms off to the side of the hall.

After asking the group to join hands in prayer and then introduce themselves to their immediate neighbors, Williamson waits for the little flurries of embarrassed laughter and murmuring to fade, and then launches into an hour-long, rapid-fire spiel punctuated by hands that chop the air and illus-trate ideas drawn from an extensive and mixed bag of sources including popular films, Jungian psy-chology, meditative slogans, personal reminiscence, environmental disasters, white-collar crime, and

Buckminster Fuller. All, however, is brought to bear on the principles of *A Course in Miracles*. Without the aid of notes or any preparation other than a few minutes prayer before she had left her West Hollywood apartment, this extraordinarily fluent speaker dazzles and moves the crowd with impeccable showmanship honed during her years as a cabaret singer; with her astonishing syntax, hilarious humor, and a rare gift to synthesize and elucidate.

"One of the things I've come to understand intellectually as a student of these things like the *Course in Miracles*, experientially as a person, and as a facilitator, is the power of ritual and acknowledging certain rites of passage," she begins briskly in a strong voice that bears only a trace of her Texas origins. "For me this night represents a shift in a personal and professional cycle."

She has figured, she says, that over nine years of lecturing for two, three, sometimes four times a week in Los Angeles, she's given over one thousand lectures on *A Course in Miracles* in that city, ("so if you think you've heard some of these things twice!") she quips, implying that "you" have.

"I've always been careful—although on some occasions I wasn't careful enough," Williamson continues more seriously, "about how much of myself I shared. I always tried to share Marianne's stories just enough to make my work cutting edge, in the sense of making it naked and raw. Just enough to help make the point, but never so much that it would get in the way, that it would become Marianne's show. I have often felt in certain places of my work, if anyone was truly listening, that there was as much in what I wasn't saying as what I was saying. There were certain things that were inappropriate to discuss because I felt they would muddy the waters of the gestalt we were all creating together."

Tonight, Williamson says, she will "open a window and then probably shut it tight"—here the audience offers an empathetic laugh—"about some things I've learned, that I would like to pass on to anyone who might be interested because they might want to carry on in their own lives some of the work we all have begun here."

She has learned so much from her successes and failures, she acknowledges, and even more "from a certain kind of community action. In the last nine years, I have truly seen it all," she says emphatically. "I've seen great heights of kindness, goodness, miracles, people behaving from their best, and I've also seen the worst that people are capable of," she says, her voice rising with emotion. "I did see an amazing thing happen in my own life," she then continues more calmly. "I did start lecturing on the *Course in Miracles* to a group of thirty-five, maybe thirty people at the Philosophical Research Society over in Los Feliz, and very slowly but surely, more people started coming. Every once in a while, I meet people who remind me that I used to serve ginger ale at every lecture. . . ." She then injects another perfectly timed note of comic relief: "At first it was old people who came, then gay people, then women, and finally, finally, straight white men did start coming." The hall explodes with laughter.

Williamson then addresses directly the unfairness of some press accounts, and acknowledges her pain at reading accusations that she is "self-promoting." She repeatedly reminds the crowd that she has never asked "you to come back and bring your friends . . . [because] I never, ever felt that my lecture was the most spiritual place somebody could be. I never felt anybody was supposed to be at my lectures except for me."

"The one thing that matters above all—and if we did it, the world would truly be changed—is that people join together and pray on a regular basis. Then miracles happen," she says. "My only job at the lecture is to prepare you for the break so then you can talk to whoever you're supposed to talk to and be in whatever place you are supposed to be."

Again, she insists upon her ordinariness. "There's nothing special about me," she declares, "and there's nothing special about my lectures. My story is not unique. If there's anything interesting about my story it is that it's *not* unique. I'm not so interested in having somebody explain to me a totally freak situation. I want someone to explain to me what I go through daily." Again the audience laughs in understanding. "I had my nervous breakdown a little earlier in the seventies than most people did," she jokes, and then notes that by being "half a step ahead," she is therefore qualified to be a teacher, according to the course.

"No," she suddenly interrupts herself. Her story *is* unique "in terms of some of the things that have happened in the last few years and what it has to say about what will be happening."

After inviting the audience to ask questions about her experience and course principles, Williamson returns to the theme of betrayal. "I have seen, I have tasted, I have experienced viciousness," she says with dramatic emphasis. "I have experienced people out to destroy you, and that's exactly what the *Course in Miracles* talks about. That is what happens in the absence of love, the ego hates love."

"If there is anything I'm proud of," she says in conclusion, looking back over the last nine years, "it's that I did hold a space for people to get together and pray three times a week." As she declares her love for her community, this model of poise chokes on her sobs.

"Marianne to me is the profoundest place of love, flowery but true," says Ellsworth. "That may be her profoundest asset and her downfall, because she can't take it all on. And she also wants love for herself."

Intense, passionate, compassionate, generous, mystical, iron-willed, sensitive, brusque, vulnerable, brilliantly funny, visionary, and, above all, loving, Marianne Williamson's story is, in a sense, our story—ordinary—and, at the same time, extraordinary, the stuff of myths.

CHAPTER TWO

BY DIVINE DESIGN

"I was born into a middle-class Jewish family," Marianne told a reporter from the *Houston Chronicle* during a recent visit to her hometown. "Our Judaism was part of everyday life in an ethnic sense, and I was taught a very Jewish approach to life. Jews tend to wear their passions on their sleeves. Jews tend to care. Jews tend to go out and get it done, whatever it is."

The youngest of three, Marianne likes to view her childhood as unremarkable, but how many fathers of normal middle-class families took their children to Vietnam on vacation so that they could experience the horrors of war firsthand? "He didn't want the military-industrial complex to eat my brain and convince me war was okay," Marianne explains in her book. Today she simply says, "That was my father. He's pretty amazing."

Sam Williamson and his homemaker wife, Sophie Ann, whose family was active in Houston charities, schooled Marianne, Jane, and Peter in a politically liberal tradition that valued learning and questioning the status quo, as well as service to the community.

Sam himself had been nurtured as a youth in a liberal, activist tradition by his father, a socialist Jew named Vishnevetsky, who immigrated from Russia to the United States via England, where he was inspired to change his name by the inscription on a passing locomotive, "Alan Williamson, Ltd." As a young man in New York, Sam had been involved with the legendary Harold Clurman and the Group Theatre. "I was twenty in 1930," Sam Williamson recalls, "and all the best-looking girls and intellectually stimulating men and women were leftists. That's where we learned to argue and have stimulating discussions. The conduit ran through me to Marianne and her brother and sister."

Houston real estate saleswoman Molly Kaplan, who is Marianne Williamson's aunt, recalls that when the children were barely old enough to walk, Sam Williamson taught them how to raise their clenched fists in a protest sign.

"My father was an armchair revolutionary," Marianne Williamson agrees. "I was raised to raise hell whenever hell needed to be raised."

"Marianne grew up around this stuff," says Sam today at age eighty-two, gesturing to the library lining his law office, pointing out a collection that includes volumes of Thomas Aquinas, the Koran, and a Hebrew New Testament. Still the fiery and humanitarian immigration lawyer, he was recently honored by the Center for Human and Constitutional Law for his lifelong work in civil rights at a dinner held at the Biltmore Hotel in Los Angeles.

The trip to Vietnam took place in 1965, after Marianne came home from Pershing Middle School and announced that her seventh-grade teacher had said if the United States didn't fight in Vietnam, the nation would be fighting communism on the shores of Hawaii.

"It so incensed my father that the public educational system was filling his children with such outrageous lies that he wanted me to see war firsthand," she says.

"I saw bullet holes, I saw orphan children. I saw terror on people's faces. I saw enough," Marianne says. "The way to breed a nation of pacifists is to take them all to a war zone for a while."

Yet Marianne received mixed signals from her parents.

"I was raised to forge a revolution," she says, "but I was supposed to do it in an organdy dress with white gloves."

Along with this contradictory legacy of social concern, passion, an inclination toward the left, and a starched commitment to propriety, a strong spiritual impulse also runs in the Williamson family. "My grandfather was very religious, and sometimes I would go to synagogue with him on Saturday mornings," Williamson recalls in her book. "When the ark was opened during the service, he would bow and begin to cry. I would cry too, but I don't know whether I was crying out of a budding religious fervor or simply because he was."

Yet Marianne hated Sunday school. "I always tell my mother I went to God in spite of my religious education."

"She's always had this religious bent," recalls Sophie Ann. "When she was a baby of three or so, I would come in to kiss her good night. Half the time she'd be sitting in bed with her eyes closed and her little hands clasped under her chin, and she'd say, 'Go away, Mommy. I'm talking to God.'"

Marianne also remembers that "I used to do a lot of pretending I was Eleanor Roosevelt," and she wondered "if the First Lady's homeliness diminished her impact as a committed humanitarian. I kept thinking, 'Could makeup have made a difference?'"

Years later Marianne would tell a reporter from the *Los Angeles Reader*, "I remember when I was a little girl, I kept thinking that something had gone wrong because I felt in my gut that the most magnificent career was to be a priest. I remember feeling perplexed, as though something was wrong. I was obviously not meant to be a traditional priest."

In most respects, however, Marianne's upbringing was normal enough to qualify for a TV sitcom. She grew up in an upper-middle-class development of identical ranch-style family homes built sturdily of brick, with spacious yards for the children, two to four bedrooms and two to three bathrooms. It was a quiet, predominantly Jewish neighborhood, a suburban oasis back in the fifties, the heyday of traditional family values. Marianne's family was one of the first to move in to what was then one of the newer suburban Houston areas, and her parents are among the few original families in the neighborhood still living there today.

The Williamsons had a "beautiful home with a little sunken den. I remember being fascinated by that," recalls Tama Walker, Marianne's friend since third grade at Mark Twain Elementary School. "Her mother was a very interesting, warm, Jewish mother, always feeding us with bagels and desserts. Marianne would have slumber parties in the sixth grade, and her father would swoop down and kiss us, pretending he was Clark Gable. It was a very dynamic household, with people always coming in and out, lots of conversation, fun arguments, and lots of life at all times."

Although most family friends point out Marianne's resemblance to her father, Walker observes that Marianne looks like neither of her parents and notes that neither her older brother, Peter, nor the middle child, Jane, were "at all like her. They weren't nearly as outgoing as Marianne," Walker observes. "They look more like Sophie. Marianne has a unique look. Her relationship with her brother and sister was the normal sibling relationship. Of course, we were off in our own little world, and they seemed remote. Jane is about two and a half years older, and Peter was quite a bit older, so he wasn't around much as we were growing up."

Beth Klein's friendship with Marianne goes back even further, to age four or five. Klein agrees that Marianne was and remains "very much like her dad.

But don't fool yourself for a minute; she's also very much like Sophie Ann. Probably in the ways she might not want to be," Klein adds, "the same ways I'm like my mother." Klein also remembers both sisters as "brazen and outspoken."

"Marianne's always been very outspoken," Klein emphasizes, "and she has been cynical in her life, believe me, as we all have been. I haven't spoken to her lately, and I don't think she would be cynical now about certain things. She's probably still cynical about others, though. There are some things about us that don't change."

The Klein sisters and their parents moved into the neighborhood across the street and three houses down from the Williamsons when Beth and Marianne were four or five. Beth, another little girl next door, and Marianne, were all the same age, and they each had older sisters who were also the same age. Beth met Marianne when the two siblings from next door and Marianne and her older sister Jane trooped over to the Klein home to complain that "our parents had built our house on the patch where they had been picking blackberries. We were ruining the blackberries that their mommies would make pies with." Beth and Jane became friends anyway, and the destroyed blueberry patch became their little joke. The four girls went to school together in a car pool. Then came Brownies, Girl Scouts, and youth groups in high school.

Even in her earliest school days, Marianne was a brilliant student and participated in many extracurricular activities. Her days were already governed by a tightly packed schedule of various educative and cultural activities: piano lessons, ballet lessons, voice lessons, acting lessons. "I'll never forget when our third-grade teacher, Mrs. Stevenson, asked us to identify a special flower she had brought to class one day," recalls Tama Walker. "Marianne was the only one who knew the answer, it was a jonquil, a flower most children in third grade don't know. That made a big impression on me. 'Gosh, she knows what a jonquil is.' "

"I remember we got in really big trouble one day when we were in the second grade," recalls Beth Klein, "because we decided we were going to walk home from elementary school. 'Oh, they're not here, so we'll just walk.' I also have very vivid memories of sixth grade, when Kennedy was killed. We sought out each other right away, because my teacher made me go stand outside because I was crying. Marianne was very upset. Marianne was always political because of her dad."

Marianne was classic teacher's-pet material: outspoken in class, better informed than her peers despite the competitive standards of Mark Twain, and totally lacking in shyness, a leader and popular with the other children.

"Our friendship was very interesting," recalls Walker. "We spent a lot of time together, and I've got lots of letters that she wrote me from all over the world, going back to sixth grade. She was always traveling. I looked at one letter the other day in which she asked me to send everyone her itinerary, so everybody could write her. I was a social butterfly too, so I would get everybody to write her at all these various places in her itinerary, such as Taiwan and Hawaii.

"In our early years, we would spend the night together and watch old movies, especially Clark Gable movies," Walker continues. "We spent hours watching the classics, analyzing them and talking about them. I still have a diary entry about spending the night at Marianne's and watching Clark Gable's *Band of Angels*. We did all the normal things you do as kids. And I went to a lot of her ballet openings. I remember seeing her when she went on toe. We played the piano together, sang together. Those are the kind of memories I have, mainly me spending the night with her, her spending the night with me, talking about religion."

Klein recalls playing games of make-believe with Marianne. "It doesn't seem like we played Mommy and Daddy that much, it seems like we played fairy tales," she says. "But I don't remember that we had a need for imaginary friends, because we had each other." Beth and Marianne also shared an interest in the dramatic that led to acting classes from the tender age of six. "One or two days a week, we would car-pool down to the Playhouse, where we first took acting lessons, and then the Alley," she recalls. "We were all involved with that. And then, of course, we were Brownies together with all the other kids."

Lenore Freedman, Marianne's acting teacher, died at the age of forty-four of leukemia, when Marianne was in the sixth grade. "Mrs. Freedman was one of those Auntie Mame characters, which always fascinated me as a child," Marianne recalls. "I loved Auntie Mame type women. She was the big actress in Houston, in Theater Inc. Her son Bobby was my first date, and Cindy Freedman, her daughter, is still in Houston, working for the Pacifica radio station."

The Williamsons were Conservative Jews and the Kleins were Reform, so the girls went to different temples on the Holy Days, but when they reached junior high school, Beth and Marianne went to temple on Friday nights "because that's when all our friends were being bar-mitzvahed," Klein says. "We would go because there were all these parties with the boys and we would get to serve the punch. Then Saturday morning we would be in religious school and then to the services afterward, and Saturday night would be the big party."

Somewhat skeptical of New Age practices, Klein does not follow *A Course in Miracles* and cannot recall any traces of a precocious spiritual bent in her childhood chum. Other qualities of Marianne's made a more lasting impression. "Marianne has always been a definite pistol," she says with a wry laugh. "She's always been very strong-willed and very intelligent. Her parents used to travel a great deal, and they would take the kids. And, of course, Marianne and Jane were always very proud of the fact that their parents were worldly. I don't remember them necessarily being braggarts, but Marianne and Jane had dolls from all over the world, and I didn't."

Walker, on the other hand, is now *A Course in Mir-*

acles student and recalls the schoolgirl Marianne as a spiritual seeker. "I was a Mormon at the time," Walker recalls. "I went to her synagogue; we often talked about our ideas about God, and we prayed a lot. I don't remember our exact ideas or what we prayed for, but that was definitely a common point. I think we just prayed to the universe. We would spend the night together, looking up at the stars and feeling at one with the universe. I carry that image strongly in my mind to this day. We had that kind of spiritual connection even back then."

If her childhood friends have slightly different impressions of Marianne, everyone certainly agrees on their memories of Sam. Extremely popular and respected within the community, Sam Williamson is a true original who has passed on to his youngest child those elusive traits we try to pin down with words like "aura" and "essence." Marianne naturally basked in the sun of her father's charismatic personality, and Sam was a hero and great influence on the neighborhood children as well.

"Marianne would go off to her various and sundry lessons," recalls Walker, "and he would pick up two or three of the neighborhood kids and take us on outings. He would take us to the zoo and point out all the unusual people there. Not the animals, but the people. He would point out unique things you wouldn't necessarily observe—different types of shoes they were wearing, the various ways they dressed. He was really into influencing young minds and trying to have you see the world differently."

Sam Williamson was also an intriguing, idealized figure for Beth Klein:

> Sam was an enigma. We used to love to go over when Sam got home. He would get his highball—he always got his highball when he got home from work—and he would mesmerize us, just by talking. My father was a doctor and Sam was a lawyer, and they were both always busy. They were good fathers, but when we got their attention, it would be a special time. I remember Sam had a convertible for a while. He would take the kids somewhere special in the car, whereas my daddy would single out my sister and I to take rounds with him on Sunday mornings and look at all the babies. We all had our special things we could do with our dads, but Sam was always interesting. The Williamsons made the news when the kids were in elementary school because Sam and Sophie Ann took the kids to India. We saw Sophie Ann all the time, so Sam fascinated us more, and as an immigration lawyer, he dealt with people who were not from this country. That was fascinating to a young child.

An impressionable and imaginative child, Marianne could easily have linked her experience of her larger-than-life father with her longing to know the Divine Father. (In fact the dedication in her book reads, "For my Father in Heaven, and my father in Texas.") The yearning for something not of this world that she felt even as a young girl could have easily been projected onto the elusive and magnetic Sam Williamson.

Walker recalls her friend as a pretty and happy child, "thin with short, cropped hair. I was looking at some sixth-grade pictures of Marianne at my birthday party," she says. "Marianne was sitting there with her arms folded, but she's smiling. She smiled a lot; I remember that about Marianne. I would say she had a pretty happy childhood. Of course, I don't know if that is what she would say."

What Marianne does say is that her elementary school days were almost as idyllic as they appeared, but life became increasingly difficult for her from junior high school on. "At the time, growing up in Houston was a painful experience," she says. Today, her brother Peter, an immigration lawyer, and her sister Jane, who teaches fifth-grade history at St. John's School, both live with their families in Houston, but Marianne thinks of the Bayou City as a good place to be from.

Marianne's present-day relationship with her parents is deeply loving and supportive. She makes it clear in her book and in her lectures that blaming one's parents is not the path toward enlightenment. But traces of the de rigueur mother-daughter friction remain to this day.

"I stayed in her house with Marianne, her mom, her baby," recalls Ellie Ellsworth of her recent visit to Los Angeles. "That was so wonderful because we were just a family. I found her mother to be charming, patient, loving, and it's so vividly clear how much she adores and admires her daughter and is very proud of her. And she's patient with her," Ellsworth adds, clearly identifying with Mrs. Williamson. "I must say I have two children and I'm very patient with them. They can be very insulting with me, but I know they aren't trying to harm me. We're the local target. It's okay. Maybe that's a little bit how Marianne is with her mom. Marianne says a lot about her past relationship with her mother. She has really worked through most of it."

Marianne never doubted her mother's love, but she chafed against the controls Sophie Ann attempted to exert on her adventurous and rebellious daughter. "My problem place with my mother was certainly not that I didn't get enough hugs," Williamson says. "She was too active with certain things. She didn't believe it was enough to love me; she had to mold me."

In a recent lecture intensive for women Marianne spoke on the need to forgive our mothers. "When we forgive Mother, that's when we see what the mother is within ourselves. It is essential to forgive your mother because that judgment turns against yourself," she explained.

Though Marianne's friendship with Beth and Tama faded for a time when the girls graduated elementary school, Marianne appeared to breeze through the transition to junior high school with ease. But in fact that is the point at which she began to feel "crushed."

As an elementary school child, Marianne was the actress in the family, doing her mom proud as she fearlessly took the stage to sing and perform in plays. But as Marianne grew older and wanted to stretch her wings, her overprotective mom sought, usually in vain, to control her adventurous daughter. Beth Klein recalls:

> When she wanted to do other things that Sophie Ann may not have been so proud of, Sophie Ann may have wanted to stop that. And Marianne wasn't fixing to let her. That's not much different than my situation, but in some cases Sophie Ann didn't want to think Marianne could do wrong. Perhaps love is blind. "I don't see my child doing something that I don't necessarily want my child to do, therefore my child's not doing it."
>
> Marianne was never bad. I did the same exact things. But she was brazen, and if she knew her mother wasn't going to like something, well, she wanted to throw it in her face. "You don't like this guy? Great! I'm going to have him over all the time, I'm going to go out with him all the time." Marianne was the baby, as was I, and I think that Sophie Ann had a hard time letting that baby go. We were kids of the sixties, so growing up was not always easy. I wouldn't trade it for anything in the world, but it was full of rebellion.

"When does the misery set in?" Williamson wonders today. "It seems misery started out for me in junior high school for the same reasons it sets in for everybody else. It wasn't just my parents, it was the times and the public education system, and Houston. One of the values of forgiving my parents," she adds, "is that once I did forgive them, I can be the effect of their strength and not just the effect of their weakness."

Despite her unhappiness, Marianne continued to excel in her classes and to shine in all manner of clubs and other activities. She even won a coveted spot on the cheerleader squad. Socially, she was equally adept. She often threw parties, and her mom and dad welcomed her friends into their home. During summer vacations, the Williamsons continued to travel around the United States, Europe, the Soviet Union, and Asia.

When Tama Walker and Marianne renewed their friendship in high school, both girls "got into some pretty heavy philosophies at that time, existentialism and that type of thing," says Walker. "But we were in different crowds. She was in the drama crowd. We kind of reconnected, but we didn't have real close connection in high school. I was more the hippie, and she was more the conservative drama student. It was funny because I went through my wild stage at that time and she was kind of conservative. Later on, she went into her wild years and I became kind of conservative. We flipped roles for a while, and we laugh about it now."

But Marianne and Walker continued to share one

long-standing common interest, the opposite sex. "We liked boys," Tama recalls. "We double-dated in sixth grade. Our parents would drop us off at the movies, amusement parks, and all that fun stuff. One of her first boyfriends in high school was president of the underground newspaper, the 'Watermelon' or something, and that was the beginning of some hippiedom. Marianne had quite a few boyfriends, and she always had a lot of style."

"I would make the C's and she would make the A's and B's," recalls Klein. "She was exactly the same. It's very funny, but I have a picture of her from the first grade and her face is the same."

In the tenth grade, the first year of Bellaire High School, Beth and Marianne both went out for an exclusive Jewish sorority. Beth was rejected, but Marianne gained easy admittance. Klein recalls:

> I was very, very hurt. Not by Marianne—she didn't do it—it was the girls who were a year older than us who decided I wasn't necessarily good enough. The deal was that the sorority girls were all very rich. 'Your friends are snobs,' my mother used to tell me, and I would fight with her over that. Then, when they didn't allow me in the sorority, I knew they were.
>
> I'm sure Marianne felt bad, because she and I were closest to each other and yet she was going to do something I wasn't going to do. That didn't happen very often when we were growing up. If Beth did it, Marianne did

it, and vice versa. But it did not change our friendship at all. We had too many other things in our lives to do.

Marianne did not remain a sorority sister for long, and like Klein, she looks back on that episode with horror: "In retrospect, that sorority is appalling to me. They're part of the sickness of that whole scene. I'll bet Beth's scarred for life, because it trains girls to be bitchy and snotty, and you choose the girls who are cool enough. She went into BBG, but it was really clear that that was not for the totally cool girls. I look back on all that stuff and instead of saying, 'Oh, it was just . . .' I say, 'How sick.' I would never want my daughter to be in something like that; they train you to judge people. And nobody said, 'Excuse me, is this healthy?' "

Sophie Ann, of course, can only remember a headstrong daughter who seemed to have things well under control. Speaking to the *Houston Chronicle*, she recalled the night when Marianne was in high school and a young man broke into the house and attacked her in her bed. The teenager was overpowered physically, but not mentally. Using only words, she was able to chase him out of her bed, out of her room, and out of the house. "Even then," her mom remembered, "she was so level-headed, so composed."

Marianne and Beth's mutual passion for theater overrode their passing interest in sororities. Bellaire had an exceptionally fine theater department attended by such future stars as Dennis and Randy

Quaid, Brent Spiner, later of *Star Trek: The Next Generation*, and Roxie Lucas, who appears on Broadway. Sophomore year, the girls encountered the first of two teachers who would exert a profound and lasting influence. "Cecil Pickett, who is a wonderful force in Houston's theater, was still teaching at our high school," recalls Klein. "Marianne and I were cast in the very first production. We were hot shit then, high cotton," Klein says with a laugh. "Because you didn't get cast right away, and we were cast in the first production. Then for Thanksgiving weekend he said, 'I would like to take a group of kids to New York City,' and she and I were chosen to be among the dozen or so who went. Had I not been through this terrible experience with the sorority, I don't know if my parents would have said I could go. Those are memories I will never forget because we stayed in hotels and we did nothing but go to Broadway shows. We saw *Auntie Mame* with Angela Lansbury, *Fiddler on the Roof, Charlie Brown*, and other shows, and Marianne and I met my sister and went to see Martin Balsam and George Grissard in *You Know I Can't Hear You When the Water's Running*.

The next year, Pickett retired from the drama department to teach on the university level. June Smith, Pickett's former student and fresh out of college, took over as Bellaire's drama teacher. Smith and Marianne struck up a deep friendship that endures to this day. "We laughed one time much, much later, when I was doing a Cole Porter musical at Berkeley," recalls Smith. "Marianne said, 'But, Junie, you were younger then than I am now.' Marianne and I have been teachers for each other in many ways," Smith acknowledges. "Right now I'm a teacher of the *Course in Miracles* myself, right here in Houston. At the time I was teaching Marianne, I was a died-in-the-wool atheist, a Jean-Paul Sartre existentialist, card-carrying atheist, Berkeley intellectual. I'm one of the miracles myself.

"Marianne turned out to be, in my eyes, a superior drama student," Smith continues. "I always found her more interesting than most of the adults I knew at the time. That's why we became friends. I knew her parents too, and once I met Sam, I understood where a lot of it came from. He's just marvelous. I had dinner with them at their home a couple of months ago. Who needs Marianne?" Smith says with a loud laugh. "He was involved with the Group Theatre, of all things, back in the thirties. He talked about Harold Clurman and said, 'We were all Reds then.'"

During Smith's first year at Bellaire, she and Cecil Pickett had a talk. "Who of your students do you think is going to make it?" Pickett asked Smith. "Marianne," she replied, but Pickett did not agree. "He was right," Smith says today, "but Cecil always looked at theatrical values, and I was responding to an intellectual intensity, a different kind of imagination. I noticed Marianne's intellect more than anything."

In her junior year, Smith says:

> Marianne stood out in a class of standout people. If I needed someone to do something

difficult, Marianne could do it. She was quite capable of stepping in and playing totally opposite roles to her type. We were doing a production of *Once Upon a Mattress*, and one of the girls dropped out of the cast because she wasn't cast in the role she wanted. That caused all kinds of ramifications. So Marianne said to me, "June, if you need me to change to another role, please do so, whatever's best for the show." That's the kind of thing I tried to promote. "We're all working together for a common cause, if you will." I look back now and realize that was one of the few times of my life when there was any joining in terms of an ensemble cast.

Marianne was scheduled to do the Queen, and she would have been just marvelous. People think it's just a ditsy, nothing show, but it's also very funny Freudian satire, and Marianne knew that. She stepped aside, took a lesser, simpler role, and she did beautifully with it. Her intellect was her strongest point as an actress; she could understand the character and had a very powerful sense of projecting that.

Years later, in *A Return to Love*, Williamson writes of returning to Houston for a reunion of her high school drama department on the occasion of Cecil Pickett's retirement from university theater. "Ex-students of his from all over the country came to pay their respects. At the dinner, a lot of attention was given to the fact that many of Mr. Pickett's students had gone on to become successful actors. But many of his students had gone on to become successful people, period. By teaching us the truth about acting, he taught us the truth about life. Once you know: (1) Leave your personal problems at the stage door; (2) Treat the material with honesty, dignity, and without embellishment; (3) Show up fully no matter how many people are in the audience, then you know everything you need to know in order to have a powerful professional career. To know the real truth about anything is to know the truth about everything. In learning the principles of ministry, we learn the principles of success, regardless of what form our ministry takes."

The summer before her senior year, Marianne made another visit to New York City and saw *Jacques Brel Is Alive and Well and Living in Paris*, Brel's theatrically conceived protest against the United States's war in Vietnam, which, at the time, had set the record as the longest-running theatrical show.

Thus inspired, Marianne decided to take up June Smith's offer to her senior students and directed and starred in her own production of *Jacques Brel*. Smith says:

> Marianne was good as a junior, but she became very valuable as a senior. I was very proud of the work she did here at the time and I continue to be. Her production of *Brel* would have done many professional direc-

tors proud. I know that sounds like a terrible exaggeration, but she did a damn good job with it. It was well-thought out, well-choreographed, and the intellectual concept behind the show was very clear. She knew exactly what she was saying, politically and socially. She was even strong enough to say when she needed help on something, instead of the usual high school "Hey, I can do it all" attitude. There was none of that sophomoric mentality with Marianne. It would be, "Junie I need help; I can't do this. What do I do?" We worked together. It's very exciting to look back on that time and the work that she did. I think she was better in her own show than in anything she did. It takes incredible intellectual concept and force of imagination to direct and act in your own show. She has much more than most of the graduate students I went to school with in Berkeley's doctoral theater program. I can honestly say I learned from Marianne. I'd never seen *Jacques Brel* before. She was lucky enough to have the family and the money to travel. Instead of froufrouing it around with sororities, she used it even then in a conscious, socially productive way.

Smith recalls that Marianne had a soprano singing voice but her "strong suit was belting a talksong. She could be in an auditorium of eleven hundred people and carry. Marianne filled it."

In high school Marianne's fascination with philosophy and metaphysics grew as strong as her interest in drama and music.

"When I was a sophomore in high school, I went to Philips Exeter one summer and took my first philosophy class," Marianne recalls. "I was very excited. It was the happiest time of my life."

"There's some points at which metaphysics and philosophy cross," Smith says, "and those are the points where Marianne and I could join. When I talked about the illusion of the cave, Marianne knew what I was talking about. We could talk about Plato together because she had learned about that not from school, but from her father."

But Marianne's high school philosophy classes had made a nonbeliever of the budding spiritualist. She "decided God was a crutch I didn't need," she writes in her book. "What kind of God would let children starve, I argued, or people get cancer, or the Holocaust happen? The innocent faith of a child met the pseudointellectualism of a high school sophomore head on. I wrote a Dear John letter to God. I was depressed as I wrote it, but it was something I felt I had to do because I was too well-read to believe in God."

As Sam Williamson's daughter and a child of the times, Marianne naturally participated in Bellaire's first student strike. "Marianne was in one particular English class—part of the accelerated college prep track—that was composed of the intellects of the school," says Smith. "They were all out there protesting, but I don't remember what they were protesting. I think it was that they wanted to wear blue jeans. It was front-page news here. I wouldn't say she was exactly radical, but I'm sure Sam was proud."

Though Beth and Marianne were constantly rehearsing a theatrical production—at least five to six nights a week for six- to seven-week periods—there was still time enough for boys. "She became involved with someone named Harold, and I became involved with someone," Klein recalls, "but I was hiding mine and she was kind of hiding hers from her mother, even though her mother knew. Her mother didn't like it. He was somewhat of a high school hero, but he was a high school hero for the left. Nobody would be right for Marianne in Sophie Ann's eyes. And that's where they had some problems. I think that's part of why she liked Harold, because Sophie Ann didn't. This was when we were just starting to be hippies, becoming aware of the drug scene, sex, and all the fun things in life. But we never got together and broke into our daddies' liquor cabinet.

"We didn't really allow ourselves to become hippies," Klein explains. "I was doing drugs at home in my parents' home, and she was probably smoking marijuana. We both smoked pot but not together. But theater was still the biggest thing in our lives. Our school was turning out more National Merit Scholars than any school in Houston.

"Then we both got out of Mom and Dad's clutches," Klein recalls. "Marianne went to California and I went to Austin."

CHAPTER THREE

MODERN WOMAN IN SEARCH
OF A SOUL

It was 1970, and Madison Avenue was already using the "winds of change" to sell deodorant and
breakfast cereals to middle America. The denizens
of San Francisco's Haight-Ashbury promenaded
down Haight Street in a mock funeral procession
cum protest of commercial opportunism. As they
mourned the death of the hippie, though, the rest of
the country's youth was just beginning to turn on,
tune in, and drop out. Marianne graduated from
Bellaire High School in 1970, just in time to join the
fun. Like most of her generation, she just wanted to
be free.

Marianne had been wait-listed at Radcliffe and
accepted at Brandeis. But she decided to enroll as a
philosophy major and drama minor at the less-pres-
tigious Pomona College in Claremont, California, an
idyllic spot in the San Bernadino Mountains about
thirty miles east of Los Angeles. "She went to Po-

mona," Beth Klein opines, "because it was as far away from Houston as she could get at the time."

"I don't know why," Marianne says. "I should have gone to Brandeis because I didn't like Pomona, but then I don't know if I would have liked Brandeis better. I think by the time I went to college, the groove of whatever was the unhappiness of my high school years was set to explode."

The summer before she experienced collegiate liberation, Marianne performed in a Cole Porter revue directed and produced by her high school drama teacher and friend, June Smith, who recalls:

> She worked with two of her good friends. One of them, Cindy Freedman, is in Amsterdam now. Her very best piece was a Cole Porter song, "Miss Otis Regrets." There was some popular country singer at the time who delivered the lyrics as if they were for real—he'd really twang it. But Marianne understood immediately that was not what the song was about. She was just marvelous, with a wonderful sense of timing. We did her up in a little black dress with a little white apron, and she performed it so terribly properly, with real insight and wit. She really cut through it. She also did a wonderfully funny song called "Find Me a Primitive Man," from a 1929 play called *Fifty Million Frenchmen,* one Porter's funniest. One line goes, "Find me a primitive man . . . I don't need the

kind that belongs to a club/but the kind that
has a club that belongs to him."

During her first semester at Pomona, Marianne
played the lead in *Toy Prison*, written by a drama
professor, Stanley Crouch, who today is a
reknowned writer and social commentator. The
character Marianne played was supposedly loosely
based on another student, Lynda Obst, who later
became a highly successful Hollywood film producer, with credits including *Adventures in Babysit-
ting*, *Heartbreak Hotel*, *Flashdance*, *The Fisher King*,
This is My Life, and presently, *Sleepless in Seattle*.
"I think Lynda Obst, myself, and probably several
others, would be different people today if it weren't
for Stanley Crouch," says Marianne today. "He's
amazing. I saw him at Emma's [her daughter's]
birthday party a few weeks ago. He has a totally brilliant mind. He was the next step after my father on
the banner of what you want to stand for on the
planet as a human being."
"That's one of the most fascinating duos, Lynda
Obst and Marianne Williamson," says Crouch with
a laugh. The character in that play was *not* based on
Obst, he says, "but it was a character that was part
radical and part naive. In fact, in retrospect, the
character now seems more based on Marianne, on
what she became. Marianne did a lot of work with
me then," Crouch adds, "and she was very good."

When I met Marianne, she was a Southern
Belle. Eastern seaboard Jews didn't really

know what to do with her because her manner and her accent didn't really fit in with what they thought was a "real Jew."

I think Lynda can't believe that [Marianne's success as a spiritual leader] happened, because Marianne was to some extent like Lynda's emotional mascot. At that time, Lynda was a very powerful figure on the campus. Very outspoken, extraordinarily brilliant, and just about the best at anything she chose to do. If she decided to go for philosophy, she became one of the best philosophy students on the entire campus. Marianne wanted to become an actress, and Lynda had overpowering charisma. She was really amazing in her ability to get people to follow her. As I recall, Marianne was in this platoon of Lynda Obst worshipers. But, at the same time, Marianne was also given to real self-esteem, though she got involved with this guy named Shelly who was kind of hostile to her. I think Lynda helped her get herself straight in this relationship, because Lynda always had a real strong leadership/maternal set of inclinations.

After the play was produced, Lynda and Marianne decided to room together during second semester. Obst recalls a more balanced friendship with Marianne. "We were really interested in each other," Obst says. "Also, we were among the only Jews at Pomona, so I think that also bonded us, that we share the psyche of Rachel. Pomona was hippie/ artsy, but it was hippie/artsy/Midwest/California/ white bread. We needed each other to match that intensity."

Though Marianne dropped out of Pomona after only two years, her time there was well-spent and typically crammed with activity, most of it purposeful. "She was pretty much the reigning star of the Pomona theater department, which is a great theater department," says Obst. "A lot of people have come out of there, like Jill Clayburgh and Robin Williams, who was at Claremont Men's College, which did a lot of shows with Pomona, and a lot of working actors you see on commercials and in movies and television."

Though Obst was the ruling campus radical, Marianne shared the same ideology and went to all the demonstrations. "The sixties broke into political animals and metaphysical animals, and we were both," Obst notes. "We were two equals, so she didn't join my thing. She went to all the rallies and was very much involved, but it wasn't what she led with. We participated in the big moratorium against the war in Vietnam and the Cambodia strike on our campus. When the kids got killed at Kent State, we shut the campus down, and she participated.

"The essence of our friendship was very much metaphysical. We used to read the I Ching together and talk about spirits and ghosts. She later claimed I turned her onto this spiritual path."

"I learned the I Ching from Lynda," Marianne

says, "and she was the one who started me on philosophy."

One night Obst saw a ghost in the dorm room:

> I woke up and was terrified. Marianne felt the shimmer of the ghost in the room and she talked me through it. She knew I had a propensity for the magical that I've subsequently denied. I didn't even remember the incident—I had suppressed it—until she reminded me. I think there was a way in which she was much more comfortable with the implications of what she was learning than I was.
>
> We all were searching for answers then, so we didn't make such a big thing about it. I later realized she was very serious. At the time, she was very metaphysically inclined and a searcher, and we would stay up all night, talking about this kind of stuff. She would find more and more original sources to think about. We were both philosophy majors, so that and theater were our deepest ties. I'd been an actress before I came to Claremont, and stopped acting in my freshman year, so Marianne became my alter ego in that respect. We had a very strong influence on each other.

Today Marianne says her college pose of the jaded cynic blocked true understanding. "I remember when I was in college, walking around with books of

Russian poetry under my arm, cultivating what I felt was a sophisticated, cynical frown worthy of my intellectual prowess," she writes in *A Return to Love.* "I felt it indicated that I understood the human condition. Ultimately I realized that my cynicism revealed very little understanding of the human condition, because the most important facet of that condition is that we are always at choice. We can always choose to perceive things differently."

But Obst, a self-described "deep skeptic and not a religious person," says that with the acuity of hindsight, she sees the nascent spiritual leader in the college girl of twenty or so years ago. When Obst finally heard her former roommate lecture on *A Course in Miracles,* Marianne's performance was the perfect fruition of that "spectacular undergraduate metaphysical education. She was really trained," says Obst. "We read Kant, Hegel, Kierkegaard, Sartre, Marx, Schiller, and she learned how to think analytically. What we most have in common is being very emotional, and for very passionate people to find the skills to articulate their feelings is a kind of liberation, but it's a kind of discipline too. We had to learn rigorously how to eliminate our emotions from our argument so we could argue truly well. That's one of the gifts a philosophy training gives you. When Howard Rosenman"—a successful independent film producer—"took me to hear her speak, I was astonished by the excellence of her sentence structure, the references, the erudition. 'Goddamn it,' I realized. 'It's that good Pomona education.' She has a really synthetic, analytic mind, and I saw her training in that area. We were both well-trained, in fact, and I think it's the secret to my success. We are both passionate, but you can't beat our arguments. We can argue, something that women aren't trained to do."

Obst also sees today signs of the woman Marianne was to become, in her youthful attraction to "lost souls and wounded puppies and people with a great spiritual need for her healing. I now see this differently, in terms of who she became, than I saw it at the time. I used to say that Marianne picked up stray mystics and I was attracted to older philosophy professors."

But Obst was not alone in her taste for brilliant, mature dons. "During college," Marianne writes in her book, "a lot of what I learned from professors was definitely extracurricular"—a sly allusion both Marianne and Obst confirm.

"Eventually we ended up double-dating philosophy professors," Obst says. "We determined at the time that the most interesting men on campus happened to be our professors in the philosophy department. I think that we were really infatuated with the subject matter. When you fall in love with a subject matter, the person who is teaching it to you becomes an intellectual transference. Mine was married, so I can't talk about him, but hers wasn't. That really brought us together too, and, of course, we wanted to be even better philosophy students."

"Philosophy professors were my weakness," Marianne jokes. "If you were a Ph.D. in Philosophy, I was easy. That's how I learned a lot of things when I was younger. I lived with a professor at Columbia for a couple of years. When I was younger, there were all these brilliant intellects around me, and I sat at their feet."

Marianne and Lynda shared other, more girlish pleasures. "We got into trouble," Obst says with a smile. "We were mischievous. If we had curfews, we'd break them. We had a lot of fun. We drove around in my red Camaro, and we used to go to Bob's Big Boy, where we'd have the same food each time. I'd have a steak sandwich with avocado and french fries with blue cheese dressing—I think she had the same thing—and we would analyze all our relationships. We still do a lot of boy talk. We actually talk about the exact same things now that we did then. We've learned more and we've fucked it up even more profoundly. It's scarier now, and *we* are scarier now as accomplished women than we were as two teenagers."

Marianne was heavier in those days, Obst recalls, and she had yet to develop her impressive personal style. "I used to have to get her to change her clothes. 'No, Marianne, get out of those.' She's really got her look together now in a way that she didn't then. She's enormously better-looking now."

After sophomore year, Marianne decided she'd received all Pomona had to offer her. "I left school to grow vegetables," she writes in her book, "but I don't remember ever growing any. There are a lot of things from those years I can't remember. Like a lot of people at that time—late sixties, early seventies— I was pretty wild. Every door marked 'no' by conventional standards seemed to hold the key to some lascivious pleasure I had to have. Whatever sounded outrageous, I wanted to do. And usually, I did."

Obst remembers no special reason for Marianne's departure, other than "it was the sixties. We have to keep this in mind. We were deeply sixties people together, as we still are in many ways, although now it's sixties in the nineties. It was a time of wanderlust and not being settled in, of moving around and finding yourself, and she was very much in the mode of doing that."

But Marianne says she left college for love. "I was madly in love with somebody who built geodesic domes in New Mexico. It was methane gas generators, solar energy, acid, and reading the Foundation trilogy," she says dryly. "I went to New Mexico, then I went to Austin, Texas. I love Austin, and I worked there as a secretary and took classes at the University of Texas."

Restless and curious by nature, Marianne was searching—though she wasn't sure for what. This period of her life, she writes in her book, was "one big personal conflagration, spent doing 'drugs and men.' I had no idea what to do with my life. I went from relationship to relationship, job to job, city to city, looking for anything that would give me some sense of identity or purpose. . . . There was some huge rock of self-loathing sitting like a pit in the middle of my stomach during those years, and it got worse with every failure. My pain deepened, and so did my interest in philosophy. . . . I always sensed there was some mysterious cosmic order to things, but I could never figure out how it applied to my own life. . . . By my mid-twenties, I was a total mess."

Marianne also recalls in her book that her favorite fairy tale as a child was "The Girl in the Patchwork Dress." A ball is to be held in the kingdom in order for the prince to select a bride. The heroine cannot afford a ball gown, so she sews together scraps of material foraged from the other girls' dresses. Embarrassed at the ball by her patchwork efforts, she hides in a closet, but the prince spies a piece of her dress peeking from the door. He opens it, and dances all night with the girl in the patchwork dress.

"When I thought of that story as an adult," Marianne writes, "I knew why it had meant so much to me as a child. It revealed a significant archetype in my own life. I would ultimately taste a little bit of just about everything life had to offer. This would never earn me a degree in anything, but it would earn me a kind of overview. That vision of things would become the basis for my career."

Drinking and drugs were not her problem; it was the "hysterical woman inside my head. My negativity was as destructive to me as alcohol is to an alcoholic. It was as though I was addicted to my own pain."

As she moved from one unhappy relationship to another, from growing vegetables in New Mexico to a few years in New York City, a few more in San Francisco, then back to New York City for another two years, working during the day in a series of jobs as a cocktail waitress and office temp in order to sing at night in cabarets, Marianne's hopes crumbled with each disappointment.

Her parents, of course, expected much more from their brilliant, high-spirited daughter, but they remained more or less supportive. "She hasn't always lived the way I would want her to live," her mother admits. "She made some major mistakes and some minor, but she has always been able to get out of them with dignity."

Tama Walker describes the relationship between Sophie Ann and her daughter during this period as "rough. Sophie just wanted her daughter to be happy the way *she* thought Marianne should be happy. 'Get it together, make money, do something, get married.' The typical mother: 'What are you doing with your life?' Especially coming from that generation, which doesn't understand this generation. We're not getting married and doing the typical, traditional things. Her mother is a very strong woman. She's very tender and sweet, but she can be very rough."

Sophie Ann theorizes that her daughter had so many avenues open to her and so many examples to follow that she was overwhelmed, and it became impossible for her to settle on one career or pick one lifestyle.

Marianne herself agrees somewhat, saying she is part of a generation that has taken too long to grow up. "As a group," she says, "we had no rites of initiation [into adulthood]. There was Vietnam, but most of us didn't fight that war." The men and women who survived World War II and went on to have children did everything they could to protect their children from life's uncertainties, Marianne theorizes. It's possible they did too good a job.

"I knew I had talent," she writes in her book, "but I didn't know at what. I knew I had intelligence, but I was too frantic to apply it to my own circumstances. I went into therapy several times, but it rarely made an impact. I sank deeper and deeper into my own neurotic patterns, seeking relief in food, drugs, people, or whatever else I could find to distract me from myself."

When Marianne came to New York City in 1973, hoping to pursue her singing career, Lynda Obst, who is a year older, was already living in New York and doing well. "In many ways Marianne would confirm that I'm a kind of big sister," says Obst. "In some ways I had more experience when I came to Pomona. So when she moved to New York she came to me in a little sisterly way too. I had just met David Obst and was hanging with a very literati kind of crowd. I was sort of in that early yuppie transition, and she was still being a struggling singer with a little bit more of a hippie thing. She came to my wedding—she was my roommate and we were historically close—but I think we felt the beginning of a real gulf between us."

Lynda connected Marianne with Albert Goldman, biographer of Lenny Bruce, John Lennon, and Elvis Presley. Marianne worked for Goldman as an assistant for approximately one year.

"I saw her every day," he says, remembering a sweet, warmhearted girl "who cried all the time" over a failed romance. "It wasn't strictly a workplace relationship," he continues, "and she worked for me as a gofer. She was very, very profoundly confused and had no conception of what to do with herself. She was a woman of emotion, like an actress in an Italian movie. I never saw her with friends. She was the last person in the world you'd think would have any success. She was always tormented, torn up emotionally. I think sheer, relentless activity must keep her together now," he opines, unable to imagine who that young girl grew up to become. "She was a sad, mixed-up twenty-one- or twenty-two-year-old who didn't know what she wanted. She flirted with the idea of being a nightclub singer, but only got on stage a few times. It was only in her mind."

"He was actually good to me," Marianne says. "I wasn't crying *all* the time. He has a good heart, oddly enough. You know how so many people in Los Angeles are wicked-hearted and pretend to be nice? Albert Goldman is nice and he pretends to be wicked.

"At that time he was doing a lot of articles for *Travel and Leisure* magazine. The main thing I did was just sit there as he talked to me with the tape recorder running. Then I would type it out. That was the way he wrote, but he would have already done a lot of writing before I arrived in the morning. But then he has a very conversational style. So I was just someone who was sitting there.

"I did that some with my book," Marianne says,

"talk to an editor with the tape recorder on and work out my ideas.

"I was very definitely a minor footnote in his life," she continues, "but he has a brilliant mind; I carry around a lot of what I learned from him, and I learned a lot about being an adult from Albert Goldman and his discipline about being a writer. I was very young and he was a grown-up. One thing that is true of me is I don't suffer incompetence and fools easily. There are a lot of children masquerading as grown-ups in our society, and it's endemic in our generation. Unfortunately, the New Thought/ New Age movement has contributed a lot to that. Regardless of what he does, Albert functions in the world as an adult and he was my first exposure to that. And interestingly enough, he treats people who work for him very well.

"One time a private call came in for me," Marianne recalls. "He knew it was very upsetting, and not only did he say, 'Take as much time as you want,' he brought me a glass of red wine. He knew people like Philip Roth and he introduced me to a very sophisticated element. He treated me with great respect. Now that I have young people working for me, I look back, and I remember that. Like Stanley Crouch, Albert Goldman was formative for me—he wouldn't know that. With the men's movement, people talk today about mentors and the master-apprentice relationship. I think I learned most in my life not from a formal education but from people I've known—and I have known several—who function in ways I want to. I think Albert fired me, but that makes sense."

Marianne's twenties were "a very tough time of my life," she says, "until I did *A Course in Miracles*." She sought help in various New Age and Eastern religions and self-help programs, lost and gained the same ten pounds, and experienced the occasional breakthrough. But nothing she found could bring lasting relief from her deep psychic pain.

In her book Marianne recalls sitting around smoking marijuana with her brother on a visit home. "He told me that everybody thought I was weird. 'It's like you have some kind of virus,' he said. I remember thinking I was going to shoot out of my body in that moment. I felt like an alien. I had often felt as though life was a private club and everybody had received the password except me. Now was one of those times. I felt other people knew a secret that I didn't know, but I didn't want to ask them about it because I didn't want them to know I didn't know."

During her first time in New York, Marianne made a brief trip to San Francisco to visit June Smith, who was now living in Berkeley. "We were going to do another Cole Porter show," says Smith. "I called Marianne in New York and I said, 'Why don't you come out and stay with us for a while? You can live with us for free and we can do this show.' Marianne picked up and left New York, and we rehearsed on the show. But it turned out that it didn't work out until after Marianne had left."

In 1975 Marianne decided to move to San Francisco. A musician boyfriend named John Timothy recalls her interest in the Ouija board, meditation, and Zen: "She had a theatrical intensity," he says.

"If she didn't like something, she *hated* it. If she felt betrayed, it was something out of Ibsen." That theatrical intensity landed her a role in a play at Berkeley. "People said they liked my singing and I should do a cabaret act," she recalls. After two years in San Francisco, she returned to New York, ready to conquer the city with a carefully crafted performance.

"I did a lot of temporary secretary work the second time in New York," Marianne recalls, "I had a six-month assignment at the New York University Law School and I worked at the Foundation for Inner Peace." (The publishers of *A Course in Miracles*.) "And I sang in clubs. I had started in San Francisco and continued in New York, at Scene One, the Duplex, the Ballroom, and a place that used to be on Seventy-second Street that I don't think is there anymore. That was how I met Jeff [Olmsted, a musician/composer]. I was not a great singer," she says. "I was a decent, good singer. I was a good performer, so people came. That's where I learned to talk to an audience. It was a very positive thing in my life and very important in terms of what I do now. I literally learned how to get up on a stage and relate to an audience."

"I went to see her perform twice," says Lynda Obst. "I didn't think it was going to work for her. You know when you and your friends are at the beginnings of your careers, and somebody plans to be a cabaret singer but you think it's not going to work? The truth was, as Marianne says, her patter—what she was saying in between songs—was more interesting than her singing. I didn't want to say to her,

'Get a day job.' I didn't know what to say, and so it sort of put a gulf between us. We ran into each other occasionally in New York, and I'd bring Stanley [Crouch] to her performances.

"It was show-tune stuff, like when you sit on a piano and belt one out. It's not my style, and in the end I think it estranged my relationship with Marianne, because you can't say to your friend, 'I don't like this.' So I backed off a little bit. It wasn't that I didn't like it; it just didn't feel like Marianne. This—what she's doing today—feels like Marianne."

Many years later, Charlotte Patton, who organizes Marianne's lectures in New York, was riding home with Marianne in a cab after she had become renowned as a teacher of *A Course in Miracles.* "She was singing this wonderful song she had written," Patton recalls. "It had kind of a rock beat; it was so powerful, and she sounded so good when she was doing it. I thought it would be so neat to just blow everyone out of the water at a lecture. I said, 'Why don't you sing at the lectures sometime?' She said, 'No, no, no, no!' 'It would be great, people would love it,' I argued, but she kept saying, 'No, no, no!'"

Without a doubt, the most significant outcome of Marianne's second stay in New York was her discovery of *A Course in Miracles* in 1977. "I first saw the course at a guy's apartment," she says. "He told me about the Skutches"—publishers of the course—"and their apartment, but I didn't go there right away."

Marianne had picked the three blue bound volumes and glanced through a few pages, but she was put off by the many references to Christ and Holy Spirit. She wasn't yet ready to receive its message, much less shape it into her own.

By 1978, however, her depression had hit bottom and she began studying the course.

"I used to get bronchitis every winter when I lived in New York," she says, "because my tonsils were never removed. I was riding the bus on my way to a doctor, very depressed because I couldn't sing with bronchitis. I passed the building where the course was published and I said to myself, 'I'm going to get that book.' That night they were on the dining room table. Jeff had gone there and bought the books. He said to me, 'I think it's time,'" she recalls, citing the Eastern adage that "when the student is ready, the teacher appears." "That night, I started reading it. I was one of those people who is a sponge to the course once they really start. I remember we looked at each other that night and we were both excited about it. I couldn't get enough of it. I was doing the workbook and the text simultaneously. By then I didn't even notice the [Christian] language."

The course message of forgiveness especially resonated for Marianne. "I never realized you can't find peace in your life without forgiving other people," she says. "I never knew how many of my problems stemmed from my fear of other people."

Marianne writes in her book of a precise, "grandiose, dramatic moment where I invited God into my life. When it came to spiritual surrender, I didn't get serious until I was down on my knees completely," she writes. "The hysterical woman inside me was in a maniacal rage, and the innocent child was pinned to the wall. I fell apart. I crossed the line between in-pain-but-still-able-to-function normally, and the real of the total basket case."

A few weeks after she had been reading and practicing the course, Marianne decided to buy it for her friend, Jamie Antoine. She went to the Skutch home, a spacious, sprawling West Side apartment that was also headquarters for the Foundation for Inner Peace, which publishes the course, and met Judith Skutch. "I said to Judy, 'I can type. If I can ever do anything for you . . .' 'I've been waiting for you,' she said. 'Would you like a part-time job?'" Judith then left to catch a plane for Marianne's hometown of Houston, where she was scheduled to deliver a lecture on the course.

"When I went home from the Skutch's that day," Marianne recalls, "I thought to myself, 'What a glorious thing to do with your life!' I remember sitting at the dining room table and saying, 'Lord, please use me.' I always remember that."

Judy Skutch traveled during that period about ninety percent of the time. Her apartment was not only home to her family, but as headquarters for the course, people were constantly streaming in and out. Though she remembers little of the volunteer office worker, she does recall that Marianne was "adorable, with really dark short hair and big eyes. She was doing the New York scene, and she wanted to sing. She was very bright, and my feelings about her were always positive. Somehow or other *A Course in Miracles* moved her very deeply, and so she attached herself for a short while as a volunteer to the foundation."

Marianne worked for the Foundation for Inner Peace in New York for over three months in 1978. After she finished the workbook, she and Jeff broke up, and Marianne decided to return home to Houston. In the summer of 1979, just before she moved to Houston, Marianne flew out to the foundation's new location in Tiberon, California, to fill in for two weeks while the regular secretary was on vacation.

Despite their spiritual partnership, the romantic aspect of Marianne and Jeff's partnership ended. Though it was extremely painful at the time, Marianne now views their relationship as having fulfilled its purpose. "I think Jeff and I were brought together to find the course," she says. "In those days, before there were lectures, it was a buddy system."

Marianne was reading the course "like a menu," as her mother characterizes it, when June Smith and her friend visited Marianne and Jeff before they broke up. "They were wonderful," Smith recalls. "They put us up in their two rooms, a typical New York apartment, and we slept on the floor." Smith recalls in particular waking from her pallet on the floor and seeing "Marianne and Jeff, outlined in the window, reading the *Course in Miracles* lesson. It was Marianne doing what Marianne did. 'It's all right, Junie,' she said to me. 'Jesus is not as bad as he's cracked up to be. It's just the people who get on him.' I thought, 'Sure, Marianne.' "

During the visit with Marianne and Jeff, June Smith also saw her former student perform in a

Greenwich Village nightclub. "It was a really nice club decorated entirely in black and white, that people would use as a springboard for their career," she says. Smith remembers the evening as a great success, with a packed audience of strangers and old friends, former Bellaire students also struggling to make it in New York. "She was singing blues, show business tunes, Judy Garland songs, what you could call high-class popular," Smith recalls. "She wasn't into a lot of rock stuff at the time."

Marianne, Jeff, and his wife Julie are close friends today, bound together by their commitment to the principles of the course.

Marianne had found in *A Course in Miracles* a tower to cleave to; it would be a source of comfort in the even more catastrophic times to come. Marianne half quips today that "a nervous breakdown is a highly underrated vehicle for personal transformation," and alludes in nonspecific terms to her own dark night of the soul—the next three years she spent in Houston—as a valuable and emblematic object lesson. "Like a lot of people in our generation, I went too far and I crashed," she explains. "For me it had more to do with men," she says, "and my own hysterical personality. My wildness and my craziness ended up having consequences. I was a bit of a Gypsy, but my dramas weren't unique. There are only a few scripts," she notes. "Anything anybody's done, I've probably done it."

Though she had adopted the pose of the wisecracking campus existentialist, when she left Pomona College, Marianne was still the innocent. As she wandered around the country, one possibility after another crumbling and vanishing, a willingness to surrender grew along with her increasing sense of hopelessness, and she felt that something greater than herself was at work. This sensing is what Jung describes as the inner snake, the knowing that one is being guided to a fateful encounter. Marianne would suffer a nervous breakdown in Houston, but it would later prove necessary, giving to her intellectual and spiritual explorations the weight and depth of true body and soul, and strengthening her character with genuine unselfish compassion, that of the wounded healer. It would make her a true teacher.

"She's not a perfect person, and I'm grateful, because she has so much to offer, and if she's not perfect, then I don't have to be," says Mimi O'Connor, Marianne's friend and former personal assistant. "Her voice is a voice in the wilderness. She came from her own devastation, and like the Phoenix rising, made something from it."

CHAPTER FOUR

THE PRODIGAL DAUGHTER

"Genesis represents the act of becoming conscious as a taboo infringement. I think that 'Genesis' is right insofar as every step toward greater consciousness is a kind of Promethean guilt. Through knowledge the gods are, as it were, robbed of their fire. That is, something that was the property of the unconscious powers is torn out of its natural context and subordinated to the whims of the conscious mind. It seems that loneliness is the vengeance of the gods, for never again can he return to mankind."

C. G. Jung, Collected Works, VII

Marianne had become an avid student of the course, but it had not relieved her deep isolation and sense of powerlessness. Marianne craved the comfort and security of her family, and in 1979 she moved back to Houston, just in time for her ten-year high school reunion.

"I went home one summer," Williamson says, "and I just realized I wanted to move back home. I was there for three years, in my own apartment. That's where I ended up having a very difficult time."

Joseph Campbell defines the shaman as "a person, male or female, who has an overwhelming psychological experience that turns him [or her] totally inward. The whole unconscious opens up and the Shaman falls into it."

Indeed, Marianne seemed to be falling deeper and deeper into the undifferentiated chaos of her unconscious soon after she arrived in Houston, and her flounderings were apparent to those around her. "The ten-year reunion was terrible for her," says Beth Klein, who had since married and moved with her husband to a town several hours from Houston. "Because she was in a very bad place in her head, she was not very happy. People were saying 'Hi, how are you doing?' and she was telling them: I said, 'Marianne, this person doesn't give a shit; don't tell them. They want to hear you go, "Fine." ' These were superficial people who didn't know her then. They hadn't cared about her in high school, so they wouldn't care about her now. I remember I put my arm around her, pulled her to the side, and—I was talking about one person in particular—I said 'Marianne, she doesn't give a shit. Don't go into detail, please.' "

Marianne's unhappiness may have spilled over the constraints of conventional social behavior, but the psyche has a wisdom of its own. Her immersion in what seemed to be a state precariously close to madness would ultimately bring her to greater consciousness. Transformation was well under way. Flooded with dark imaginings, fantasies, and dreams relieved only by the occasional glimpse of enlightenment, Marianne was also engulfed by a pervasive sense of her own peculiarity, of being out of touch with ordinary reality and everyday people.

"The gods express themselves through our wounds," Jung notes. Marianne was coming face-to-face with her own wounds, but it would be the source of her future revelations. By addressing those wounds, she was becoming more aware of her humanness, her divine limitations, and her need of others—God and people—in a different way than she had previously experienced. Marianne was still making her men into gods, but that impulse and the pain that followed each inevitable realization that they were, after all, merely men, was the forerunner of true faith, the beginnings of her realization that what she longed for would not necessarily be found in material form.

In the midst of her growing despair, Marianne fell in love with a businessman from out of town named Larry McGinty and impetuously decided to marry him. "It was a spur of the moment thing, a whirlwind romance that didn't last long," says Tama Walker. The marriage lasted, according to Williamson, "for a minute and a half." The couple split, her mom comments wryly, before she'd received all the wedding bills.

Beth Klein could not attend the large, traditional wedding, but she tried to stop her friend from what she considered a rash decision:

> I met him twice. He seemed very pleasant. I knew in my heart it wouldn't work, but she saw it in the cards. I think California made her mystical, and for her, it was in the stars that she would marry him. I said "Marianne,

I love you so, but you're out of your mind!"
She didn't know him. As far as I was concerned, her life was revolving around someone else. But when Marianne gets something
into her head, you're not going to tell her
anything different. The marriage didn't last
because Marianne was at a very unhappy
place in her life. I told her she was manic-
depressive, "Get out of this."

After her marriage broke up, another relationship
failed, and Marianne finally bottomed out.

"I had a huge conflagration over a relationship I
never talk about," she says, "and that's when I
ended up having a nervous breakdown; it was the
most formative and the worst period of my life. In
retrospect, it turned out to be the best period of my
life. Andrea McDermott [a Houston friend] said to
me at that time, 'I know you do not believe this, but
one day you will see this as a good thing.' It was
true. I wrote in my book that many people have a
number of small nervous breakdowns, but I'm glad I
had a big one. I felt I had exploded into many different pieces, and when I came back, I felt I wasn't the
same person."

During her three-month marriage Marianne had
started a New Age bookstore with McGinty's help.
She had returned home to discover a changed city.
"In some ways Houston lost its charm, but in
another way it gained sophistication," she told a
local reporter. "I like Houstonians. I'm a native
Houstonian. Houstonians think big." Big enough,

Marianne thought, to welcome a sophisticated Greenwich Village–style bookstore/coffeehouse/ cultural salon which would be a gathering spot for local intelligentsia and truth seekers.

"I had this bookstore/coffeehouse, and I was still singing," she says. "You see now how each thing relates to the other. What does a person do who works with books and sings? Oh, she becomes a professional talker on books!"

The Heights Bookstore, named after its location in an out-of-the-way part of Houston—which, unfortunately, would eventually doom the project—provided a much-needed opportunity for Houston's artsy intelligentsia to rub elbows. "I have one customer who comes into the Heights Bookstore who's writing a novel, but he doesn't know anyone else who's trying to do the same thing," Marianne told a reporter from the *Houston Post* in 1981. "He *should* know other novelists—they could help each other."

Even at this point in her life, Marianne's willingness to serve the community at the highest level possible dominated the profit motive. She recalls in her book:

A man came in one day and told me that he was going to teach me how to make money. "Every person that walks in that door," he said, "is a potential sale. And that's what you should silently say to yourself whenever a customer walks into that store: Potential sale, potential sale."

His advice sounded exploitative to me. He

was advising me to view other people as pawns in my own scheme. I prayed and received these words: "Your store is a church." Church, esoterically, means the gathering of souls. It's not an outer plane but rather an inner plane phenomenon. People don't come into your place of business so you can *get* anything. They're sent so that you can give them love.

After I said the prayer and got the feeling that my store was a church, I understood that my only job was to love the people who came there. I actually did that: every time I saw a customer walk in, I would silently bless them in some way or another. Not everyone bought a book every time they came in, but people began to consider me their bookseller. Customers were attracted to a peaceful feeling in the air. People might not know where it comes from, but they can feel it when love is being sent in their direction.

A Course in Miracles was in abundant supply in the Heights Bookstore. If customers wanted, she would tell them what she had deciphered thus far.

Browsers were clearly welcome, even encouraged. They could nestle in fluffy pillows or relax on a wicker love seat to thumb through books or peruse the many news sheets. The store was filled with such homey decorator touches as plants, colorful wall hangings, and tablecloths. A large old dictionary was kept handy, along with a few of Marianne's own favorite books. Coffee or tea was available, and an area was marked off for youngsters to busy themselves with crayons and coloring books or children's literature.

Marianne ordered the books herself and prided herself on the store's stock of such unusual publications as *Red Star Over China* (written in Chinese) and *Cherokee Cooklore,* which couldn't be found in "regular" bookstores. Her selection was small but eclectic, covering subjects ranging from art and cooking to Texas history and general fiction. She also included a large selection of children's books, and stocked greeting cards, wrapping paper, and an array of albums recorded by female artists. The bookstore was pure Marianne—full of works on religion and philosophy and without the popular junk novels of the day. "Let people go to the drugstore if that's what they want," she told her mom.

Marianne had created the perfect atmosphere for informal lectures and discussion, and an excellent place to meet interesting people. She quickly acquired a clientele ranging from young professionals who had recently moved into the Heights area, to old-timers who had been in the neighborhood for years, to persons from surrounding areas who simply stumbled upon the store.

"Socially, you're not allowed to talk to someone sitting next to you in a bar or a restaurant without it carrying all kinds of implications. But that isn't so in a bookstore," she told the *Post.*

The Heights Bookstore became a place where interested people could have a different kind of fun.

Typically, Marianne used her place as a venue for a wide variety of organized activities. She brought groups together for lecture series and other informational and cultural events. The lectures and readings gave local writers, poets, and speakers an outlet for their work.

The Houston-Arts Club started with about thirty-five bookstore regulars. To kick off the inauguration, Marianne promoted a program called "Something for Valentine's Day: Songs that Melt the Heart," at a popular Houston venue, Rockefeller's nightclub. Backed by a five-piece band called the Little Egos, she performed standard love songs and a few modern pieces.

The bookstore also was home to programs such as "Political Patchwork: a Monthly Political Lecture Series," and "Houston Humanistics: a Monthly Humanities Lecture Series," with speakers representing widely varied points of view and experience. They included the Houston city comptroller, a member of the Democratic national convention, the chairman of the Harris County Moral Majority, and an expert lecturer on Egypt. Another program, the "Houston-Arts Reading Series," was held in conjunction with the University of Houston creative writing division, from three to five P.M. on the first Sunday of each month. Selected fiction writers and poets from the Houston area read their works. "Whippersnappers Workshop," a program of arts, crafts, stories, and songs for children of all ages, was held from three to five P.M. every Sunday.

One of the most popular programs at the store

was "Torch Song Sundays," in which regular customers would come to the store on Sunday mornings to read *The New York Times* over bagels and
cream cheese, while Williamson and a pianist performed torch songs from the thirties and forties.

"Culture should not be just for the rich," Marianne declared to a local news reporter. "It's enough
that it's just for the organized."

Tama Walker and Marianne had reconnected at
their ten-year high school reunion, and at twenty-
eight they'd regained the closeness they had enjoyed
as elementary school children. Walker recalls:

> Marianne was writing these wonderful songs
> all the time and singing them to me. They
> were her own unique style, a kind of mix of
> folk and rock. I always thought she'd be a
> great songwriter. I was recently looking at an
> old tape of the songs she'd written that she
> sent me from L.A. when she first got there in
> 1983 or so. I remembered her singing them
> to me and how much I liked them. The
> themes were all about men: "When I Think of
> You, Darling"—that was one of my favorites
> —and "He Might Call." I wanted her to go to
> L.A. and become a songwriter.

Andrea McDermott, another childhood friend who
reconnected with Marianne, recalls such titles as "I
Recall You Angel," "Toyota," and the following lyrics
from another song whose title she cannot recollect:

He left this morning,
took the truck to Santa Fe.
He didn't mean to wake me up,
but I just work that way.
How can I sleep when deep inside
I can tell he's gonna leave now?
He says, "I might as well."

In addition to her inaugural performance for the Houston-Arts Club and Torch Song Sundays in her bookstore, Marianne was making the occasional appearance at local nightclubs, still nurturing hopes of a singing career.

"The last time I saw Marianne perform was at a fashionable club here in Houston called Rockefeller's," says June Smith. "She was marvelous. She did a beautiful thing, the only specific thing I can remember. The band was onstage in low silhouette and Marianne came out in darkness. Before there was any light on her, you heard her start, 'I feel a song coming on . . .' and the lights came on with it. It was a brilliant theatrical moment."

"She was singing in local nightclubs here while she was running her bookstore," says Tama Walker. "She did all the art work for posters and postcards advertising her performances." Despite her efficient management of a typically hectic schedule running the bookstore and the various clubs, and singing, Marianne was steadily falling apart. "She was busy even though she was torn up and emotional at that time. It was all men. Of course, we talked a lot about that," Walker says, and continues:

She was having a tough time in Houston, but the bookstore was very effective and it brought a lot of people together. We'd never had anything like that in Houston before and we don't have anything like that now. It was quite unique. People would just hang out there, drink coffee, and talk. She brought a lot of people in to speak, including Mercedes McCambridge, who did the voice for *The Exorcist*. . . .

Marianne was heavy into the course, and she got me into it. I'd go over to her apartment and she was using the books so much that they were all torn up. She had been self-studying it for two or three years by then. She didn't try to [start a study group], but she was just offering information. I think it was keeping her sane. She was going through a lot of things at that time. She married, got divorced, ran the bookstore—a lot of responsibilities. She was out there putting her life on the line like she does now, challenging everything, and launching quite ambitious projects. The course kept her peaceful, and she certainly brought a lot of people into it at that time.

But Marianne was straddling the spiritual fence, indulging in occasional recreational drug use to dull her pain; at the same time, she was studying a discipline that obviously would guide her toward confronting her issues with clarity and working them through. Walker recalls:

> She did the typical "Let's get high and forget about our pain." But even then, there was something unique about the way she did it. We would go to people's houses—I didn't get high at the time—but they were getting high, drinking and all this kind of stuff. Marianne would sit down and say a prayer for the situation. She was constantly praying and asking for help, all through the eighties. "Is this for real?" I would wonder. She was getting high and praying, and I thought, "This is really wild. Is this a dream?" But it was great. Looking back on it, I realize that was really quite unique, and then, of course, I see where she is now. Even now she helps me if I call her with a problem. "Let's pray about it," she'll say over the phone, and it's a lot of comfort. She's a great companion, an absolutely wonderful friend; she'll do anything for you.

"I've had the experience of being on the floor," Marianne said once in a lecture, "the kind where you're already seeing a psychiatrist five times a week but you still need an extra push if you're ever going to get up. That period of darkness completely informs what I do now."

"My friend Buzz tells me you're crazy," Sophie Ann Williamson informed her daughter one day.

"Your friend Buzz is right," Marianne replied.

"My friend Buzz tells me we should send you to a psychiatrist," Sophie Ann countered.

"That would be helpful," Marianne said.

"But," Sophie Ann insisted, "I want a good Jewish M.D. psychiatrist. I don't want any of this New Age, Christian, *Course in Miracles* stuff. A Jewish doctor!"

"Fine, anything!" Marianne agreed.

"So she came back to me," Marianne recalls, "and she said, 'I found him, and he's married to Lulu Weingarden . . . and he's good, and . . .' So I went to see this guy. Now this is in 1980. You think this was before I got into the *Course in Miracles*? No! Right after finishing the workbook!

"So I went to see this guy in Houston, Texas, 1980," she continues, "and I said, 'I should tell you something before we begin. I wanted professional help and I've come see you specifically because my mother said you were a Jewish doctor, but you need to know that I'm a student of a set of books called *A Course in Miracles*. If you're going to work with me, and you do anything that goes against these books, it absolutely will not work because they mean everything to me, blah, blah, blah. If you're going to tell me it's the course's fault, and blah, blah, blah.' And this Jewish doctor from Houston in 1980 looked at me and said, 'I've done the course.' I think that's pretty amazing.

"That man put my life together," Marianne continues. "I felt at that time like a Greek vase that had been painted and someone had dropped on the floor. It was shattered into a thousand different pieces. That's how you feel when you really fall apart. Most people would say, 'Well, it might have been worth something, but forget it now. It's completely shattered.' That man painstakingly glued every piece back together."

When Marianne returned to Houston twelve years later for a book-signing, her former psychiatrist was there to greet her. "An incredible man," she says. "I don't know where I'd be today if it weren't for that psychiatrist."

Marianne had other help as well. "You know the story *Snow White and the Seven Dwarfs*," she begins. "Snow White goes to sleep and these little people take care of her. I experienced that when I had my nervous breakdown. I had this little group of people I would never have noticed before, a girl named Pattie Wilson and a guy named Raphael. It was like Snow White and the Seven Dwarfs; they were physically unattractive. They helped me at the bookstore; they did it for me. To this day it's almost like I think maybe they didn't really exist and God sent them. I had this bookstore but I was a mess. That's when I really *was* crying all the time. My entire career was born of that period. You know when you give something to somebody and they say, 'I'll pay you back when I can.' I'll say, 'No, someday you'll give to someone else.' So much of what I have done in my life is to pay them back.

"That's why I talk a lot in my lectures about people who take care of people being put down today as enablers," she continues. "Sometimes strong people are not chronically on the floor, they just fall down at times. What would I have done if those people hadn't taken care of me? I would not be here today. I look back and wonder, 'Who were these people?' The interesting thing is, I was down there with them. So who am I kidding? They were in the gutter and saw me as one of them. What I learned is the camaraderie of those in the gutter. But they seemed to know I didn't come from the gutter. I didn't belong there, and they were going to bandage me up and send me back into the world."

Actress Melanie Chartoff recalls a gathering years later in Los Angeles when Marianne was trying to raise money for the children of drug-addicted men and women:

> This was my favorite speech she ever made. I can't remember the whole thing, but the gist of it was, "There was a time in my life when people turned away from me." And she started to cry, which was amazing to me. I'd never seen her lose it. She said, "There was a period when I was in terrible need and trouble and people turned away, and then there were a couple of people who didn't. If it wasn't for them, I might not be here now." I just started crying too. It was·the first open admission of why helping people is so important for her. It was a "there but for fortune go

I' kind of speech, so from the heart and so vulnerable.

During her last lecture in the early summer of 1992, a questioner asked Marianne, with the urgency of a child requesting a favorite fairy tale, for the "Jesus at the cocktail party" story. Marianne demurred, she didn't want to tell it again. But she gave in and did.

"So I had a nervous breakdown," she began matter-of-factly. "I've written about it. One of the themes of these lectures is you never know what people are experiencing at four-fifteen A.M. What I learned is everybody has those four-fifteen A.M. moments. So everybody deserves your compassion more than you know, because if you've had one of those nights, people should be nice to you forever. When I was lying there unable to sleep, I began to sense a presence at the end of my bed. It felt like a tall male, upright, just sitting on my bed. It never felt like anything to be afraid of. It felt real, and it was an amazing thing happening in my life. I stared, wondering who it was. It began to dawn on me that this warmth in my chest was Jesus. There were no words, nothing but this incredible warmth I felt. You could be saying 'She's crazy,'" Marianne interrupted herself, and then injected a note of comic relief. "That is an option. You have to consider that every once in a while, because it keeps you humble."

During this period, Marianne was seeing her psychiatrist five times a week, but "I wasn't getting any better," and she was terrified. "I was not normal and I knew it," she said. "So I said to Jesus, 'Look, if you can give me back my life, if you can restore me somehow, then I will do whatever you want me to do for the rest of my life.' Like people make a pact with the devil, I made a pact with Jesus."

Marianne began having a stronger sense of His presence, "and slowly but surely, I got better. That was a three-year dark period, and Jesus became very real to me. It's a matter of faith, but for me, it was very true—I felt the guy on my shoulder.

"I started getting better, but I wasn't so comfortable with his presence there," Marianne went on. "I started thinking things like 'Jesus, thank you. I really appreciate everything you've done for me. I get that you were there for me during very dark times. I appreciate everything you've done, but I'm really fine now. I think there are probably other people who need you now.' "

One night Marianne went to a "fancy cocktail party." At the party she wandered into a room where men were conversing in small groups, drinks in hand. "I don't know if it was a spontaneous hallucination, a vision, a waking dream, whatever, but I saw these two guys," she said. "I was going to say 'Hi!' when I realized that one of them standing there, all dressed up, was Jesus. This wasn't a feeling; this was a spontaneous hallucination of some sort. It *was* Jesus. He turned around and he looked at me. His eyes were focused on me, and it was like someone looking straight into my soul. There was no judgment, no sarcasm, no edge, but he said to me very clearly, very plainly, 'I thought we had a deal.' That's my Jesus at the cocktail party story."

Marianne had planned to convert the Heights Bookstore into a children's bookstore and cultural center and move the books for adults to another location where she could manage a restaurant/bar in conjunction with a late-night bookstore, modeled after a similar operation in Washington, D.C., called Kramer Works and Afterwords.

She remembers sitting in her bookstore one day in 1983, thinking that she would stick around for "a long, long time. Then I got a flash that I wouldn't be there long at all. Then I got an added flash that I was going to L.A. It surprised me."

She left soon after, barely locking the bookstore door behind her. "What was I going to do in L.A.?" she asks rhetorically. "I had no idea."

"She wanted to sing or do something like that out there," Walker recalls. "She called me one day and said she was moving to L.A., and then packed up what she wanted from her apartment and moved within a week or two. I wasn't surprised because she had done what she could here, and I don't think Houston was happening enough for her. The bookstore was a great idea, but Houston wasn't ready for it. And I think she was meant to move to L.A."

"It wasn't a peaceful time," Marianne comments today, "but I learned a lot."

Marianne left Houston for Los Angeles with everything she owned in her mother's car and not much of a plan in her mind. She wasn't sure why she was going. She just knew it was time. "The truth of the matter is, I didn't have courage. I was completely naive," she says. "When you sort of don't have anything, what have you got to lose?"

CHAPTER FIVE

THE COURSE

A Course in Miracles is not a religion but a system of thought. It describes itself as a self-study course of spiritual psychotherapy. "It is one of many paths home," explains Pat Buckley, a psychotherapist based in New York City. "It is not the only one, but it does promise to save you time. The goal of the course is not to die and leave this world, but to live in this world with inner peace. *A Course in Miracles* is a gentle undoing of the ego, a removal of the blocks to our peace and happiness."

At its simplest level, the course integrates psychology and spirituality. People may try to accomplish some of the same goals others seek in psychotherapy or other personal and spiritual growth experiences, although many psychotherapists who practice the course do not consider it a substitute for therapy. On a more mundane level, practitioners say it offers a practical way to live, to deal with personal issues and to understand life from a different perspective.

"The *Course in Miracles* isn't about making happen whatever you want to happen," Marianne reminded an audience in the summer of 1992, as she looked back over her nine-year career. *"A Course in Miracles* is about asking that God's will be done," she emphasized. "You always want to remember the difference between magic and miracles. Magic is when you give a shopping list to God. Magic is when you say, 'God, I want this to happen, this to happen, and this to happen.' A miracle is when you say, 'God, what can I do for you?' Big difference. I've seen that in my professional and personal lives. In the areas where I do that, everything is fine; the areas where I don't are a problem.

"Resistance to goodness is what the *Course in Miracles* calls the ego-mind," she continued. "That's what I've been talking about for years, and that's what the course is all about—the incredible force field that would tempt us to deviate from love. It is not only active in our own minds, but, most importantly, it is active in the collective mind. It is active in the collective projections."

According to its publisher, the Foundation for Inner Peace, *A Course in Miracles* has sold more than 800,000 copies worldwide to date, with no greater concentration of sales in any one part of the United States. The foundation publishes fifty to sixty thousand copies each year.

A representative for the Bodhi Tree, Los Angeles' largest and best-known bookstore for spiritual and

New Age material, reports that even before the publication of Williamson's *A Return to Love,* sales for *A Course in Miracles* averaged nearly twenty per week —a large number for a book that has virtually no advertising and has been on the market for more than ten years.

The course was "written down" or "scribed" by an atheistic psychologist in her mid-forties named Helen Schucman. She came to believe the voice of Jesus was directly dictating to her. Schucman worked in the psychology department of Presbyterian Hospital at Columbia University's College of Physicians and Surgeons amidst a contentious and stressful professional environment. "There must be a better way and I'm determined to find it!" Bill Thetford, the department head, burst out to Schucman one day. Schucman pledged to help her colleague, thereby unleashing a series of disturbing psychic experiences in which she seemed to "know" things she wouldn't have known through normal means. Gradually she came to recognize an inner voice that spoke to her. One night in 1965 Schucman phoned Thetford, frantically complaining that the voice wouldn't leave her alone. "It keeps saying, 'This is a course in miracles. Please take notes.' " Schucman thought she was going crazy, but Thetford advised that she do what it ordered.

Much has been written about the relationship between Schucman and Thetford concerning their conflicting personality styles, Thetford's position of authority over Schucman, Schucman's unrequited attraction to the younger man, and her frustration at not being able to control him sexually. But those were mere undercurrents. Deep love, integrity, and commitment came to overrule what was often a prickly interaction.

With Thetford's help, Schucman began listening to the voice and recording its words in shorthand. Each day, Thetford would help her, often holding the terrified woman as they transcribed the notes—statements of universal truths and practical lessons to replace ego-controlled fear with unity and love—into typewritten form. The process began in 1965 and lasted seven years. The voice Schucman heard identified itself as that of our self-described "elder brother," Jesus.

"The voice of Jesus is subject to interpretation," says Bob Skutch, who publishes the course. "No one can prove anything. It's all a matter of belief and faith. If you believe in the survival of consciousness, the voice could be Jesus. You could believe it was something else."

Yet for other course interpreters, the acceptance of Jesus as the author is essential.

"Many students of the course compromise by ignoring Jesus in the course and focusing in the Holy Spirit," notes the newsletter published by Kenneth and Gloria Wapnick's Foundation for *A Course in Miracles*. "But it is extremely important not to forget that the whole purpose of the course is to help us, first and foremost, to look with Jesus at the *interferences* to God's Voice, and not simply to hear specific instructions from on high."

"In the case of Jesus, the problem isn't as simple as coming up with another word," Marianne writes with humorous practicality in her book. "Jesus is His name. There's no point in pretending that His name is Herbert."

Embarrassed by the manuscript and fearful that it would damage their academic reputations, Schucman and Thetford did nothing with the course for a few years. In fact, Schucman was not publically revealed as the "author" of the course until after her death in 1981. The result of her and Thetford's efforts, and the work of others who later helped edit and ultimately publish the course, is the 1200-page, three-volume text, *A Course in Miracles* (Foundation for Inner Peace $40).

Gradually Schucman and Thetford had shown the manuscript to a few people. Kenneth Wapnick, who had been considering a life spent in retreat from the world, was introduced to the pair through Father Michael, a mutual friend. After a long trip to Israel during which he became increasingly eager to see the "book" Schucman and Thetford had "written," Wapnick returned to New York and became the main editor of the course. He has devoted his life to its study. Judith Skutch and her former husband Bob became its publishers.

To the casual observer, Skutch's life was full of meaning. She was happily married, with two interesting children, and she enjoyed a wonderful relationship with her parents. She taught parapsychology at New York University and, with her husband, ran the nonprofit Foundation for Parasensory

Investigation. Her home, a spacious apartment located in the Beresford, at One West Eighty-first Street, was a salon for people interested in parapsychology and new dimensions in healing. "My daughter reminds me that once she got up and went fuzzily into the kitchen for breakfast. A man was sitting there, reading a newspaper," Skutch says. "They said 'How do you do?' She said, 'My name is Tamara, I live here.' And he said, 'Well, my name is Stuart, I've been living here for a week, too.'

"That's what it was like."

But Judith Skutch was troubled by "an emptiness," even though her life seemed totally full:

There was still something missing. I couldn't put my finger on it, and I didn't know where to look, so I looked in some silly places. One day I was suddenly taken by a really profound sense of void. I locked myself in my bathroom that afternoon when no one was in the house and I began screaming, "Won't someone up there please help me?!" I meant it. A few days later, I met Helen, Bill, and Ken. I thought it was just another meeting with just some more people, until I sat in their office and they told me the story of how the course came to them. There wasn't any question in my mind. I had known these people. I didn't know where or how, but it was as if I had suddenly "grocked" them; it was a connection that went beyond words. I couldn't have told you about their lives or about their thoughts; it was more of a feeling of identification that I had been with them before. Even then, I wasn't too sure what that meant.

You can call it function, assignment, life's work, whatever. There's no question in my mind that I had been desperately asking for something meaningful in my life. I think it was immediate recognition on my part that this would be it for the rest of my life and nothing else, which was very comforting, like meeting a guy who you know you will be with forever.

According to some who knew her, Schucman was disappointed in the failure of her remarkable experience to impact significantly on her personal life; in other words, to make her blissfully happy for the rest of her days. When Willis Harman, president of the Institute of Noetic Sciences, asked Schucman why she herself did not seem to have benefited from the unusual document that had brought peace to so many others, Schucman replied, "I know the *course* is true, Bill, but I don't believe it."

Roger Walsh, professor of psychiatry and philosophy at the University of California, Irvine, and author of books on comparative religions, met Schucman in the seventies and investigated the claims she made about writing the course through channeling. He says he found Schucman's story believable, in that he was sure she really believed she was writing through a voice which was Jesus Christ.

"I believe she was accessing a very profound part of her mind from which some profound insights emerged," explained Walsh. "Schucman was embarrassed by the whole affair. She was very uptight, like the rest of us. I think she would have been much happier not to have done this. She briefly worried that she might be psychotic when she first had the experience."

But Walsh met Schucman at an early point in her experience with the course. Judith Skutch, who was very close to her, remembers Schucman differently: "I knew Helen was my great teacher. It wasn't even thought; it was a given. She wasn't companion, she wasn't Mother. So I had emotions connected with Helen that a lot of people who met her didn't have, meaning you like to please your teacher and do well for your teacher."

While Skutch acknowledges that Schucman was perplexed by her experience, "she was the perfect vehicle to do what she did, because she did it. She did it without interference. She didn't rewrite it; it wasn't something she would have written herself, on her own. When I took *A Course in Miracles* home with me, and during the subsequent meetings with her, there was no question in my mind whatsoever: had she written this? Was this a big con? First of all, why would it be a con? They weren't asking me to do anything. And they were very embarrassed about giving it."

Judith Skutch had met Schucman and Thetford in 1975:

I think they recognized by this point something had to be done with it. There was no one around they could tell; there was no way they were going to a publisher saying, "We think this should be published." They didn't want to be connected to it because they didn't feel they were the proper representatives of the material. The material was for students, and they couldn't represent themselves as having accomplished it. They both felt they had done their jobs by taking it down. It was a very long and tiresome period, they gave their all to it, and I think when I came along they were wondering, "What are we supposed to do with this?" They had asked the voice, as they had asked the voice about everything, what they were supposed to do with the material, and were told that someone was going to come along and take it on its way. This went on for a few months. When they asked again, the answer was, "She is not ready." I seem to remember when I asked Helen the "Why me?" question, she said, funny, she had asked that of the voice and it said, "Because she is now ready for her spiritual education." That is exactly what I was ready for, and no other answer would have been meaningful to me.

No one at this point considered publishing the course. Schucman, Thetford, Wapnick, and Skutch simply met at the Skutch apartment daily for two or three hours to study the course for over two years. Judith gradually began lecturing on course principles, until finally the group arrived at the next natural step: to share the course with the public. Judith and Bob Skutch formed a publishing company, and in 1977 a Foundation for Inner Peace ran the first printing of *A Course in Miracles*.

The text is tough reading, seeming even disjointed at times, and the philosophy can be confusing in that it is not technically a form of Christianity, but uses redefinitions of Christian symbolism, themes, and metaphor—albeit redefined according to the course point of view—as well as reconceptualized Freudian terms such as "resistance," "projection," and "ego." Yet the difficulty in explication forces the student to spend more time with the concepts, and thereby affords the opportunity to deepen understanding. In their basic form, the course precepts aren't truly difficult to grasp, at least on an intellectual level.

The course is predicated on the reality of the spirit, rather than the body. The material world is illusory, it teaches, created not by God, as is commonly held by the religions of the world, but *by man as an attack upon God.* Only love is real, it says. That concept is meant to be taken strictly literally.

"Biblical religion would say God created the world," says Kenneth Wapnick, "whereas the course says not only did he not create the world, he doesn't know it exists, because if he did know, then it would have to be real."

In a personal sense, the crux of the teaching is that each person's relationship to God has never been impaired, Wapnick says. "It is a cornerstone of Christian theology that Jesus suffered and died for our sins," he explains. "But he makes it very clear in the course that he did not suffer, and that the crucifixion was a way of teaching the world that the so-called sin against the love of God has no effect and was only a dream."

The source of human unhappiness, says the course, is our erroneous sense of separation derived from the illusion of our bodies. This illusion leads us to judge and condemn others, and to become fearful and defensive.

"When we have it straight," explains Pat Buckley, "we go to the movies and we know the projector is behind us with the film. The screen is just being projected upon. If something goes wrong with the film, we don't run up to the screen and try to fix it. We run back to the projector and film. But in life, we have it all backwards. We run out 'there,' to that screen called the world. We try to fix it out 'there,' forgetting that the projector and the film are within us. We know what we're doing in the movie house, but we don't know what we are doing when we get out of the movie house."

The notion that the world doesn't really exist and was literally made as an attack on God is perhaps the most threatening course concept. "Many compromises have been attempted by students, even unto ignoring the premise itself because of the great discomfort that it engenders," notes the newsletter of the Foundation for *A Course in Miracles.*

This idea is "bound to arouse terror in the part of our minds that identifies with this thought and the guilt that must inevitably arise from it," the newsletter continues. "Furthermore, a radically different spirituality, worldview, and mode of being in the world would occur with the total acceptance of the thought that the world and the body are illusions and therefore were *not* created by God. Rampant resistance to a Course without compromise is therefore understandable and inevitable. . . ."

One explanation for the resistance, the newsletter goes on to explain, is if God didn't create the material universe, then He can't be blamed "for our personal, interpersonal, transpersonal concerns, let alone our social, political, economic, and environmental problems. . . ."

Another reason for this resistance is "if we were to accept that the world is illusory and therefore not real, then we who believe ourselves to be part of this world, encased in a body with a distinct and special personality, must also not be real. Anxiety! Alarm!"

Its very existence challenged, the ego launches a "last-ditch stand . . . If I am to exist as a special creature, autonomous of God, then there *must* be a world and body to house my specialness, not to mention a special 'God' and 'Voice' to affirm this specialness for me in front of others."

Judith Skutch tells the story of a friend, a well-known dress designer in New York, who had been studying the course avidly for three or four years. He would visit the foundation headquarters and discuss the course with Helen Schucman, Bill Thetford, Ken Wapnick, and the Skutches. He felt the course had changed his life; he gave away countless copies, and even took a long vacation just to study it. One day he called Judith from a place outside this country. "You have to correct a major error in the course in the next printing!" he shouted excitedly over the phone.

"What are you talking about?" she asked.

"There's a major error in it," he persisted, "and you haven't noticed it? I can't believe it!"

"Tell me what it is," Judith urged. "We do have erratas, misspelled words, periods, and capitals that shouldn't be there. Tell me what it is."

Then he said, " 'God did not make this world, you did.' "

"That's right," Judith answered.

"No!" he insisted. "That's wrong!"

"Well," Judith said, "What do you think it should be?"

He said, *"God* made this world, *you* didn't." It wasn't an error, and the man dropped out.

The foundation newsletter explains:

> Because *A Course in Miracles* goes directly against everything the world believes, it would be next to impossible for any sincere student not to experience resistance to its message in some manner. . . . If one feels no resistance, and is able, for example, to

hear the Holy Spirit with crystal clarity, then either the person is so spiritually advanced that the Course is superfluous, or else is filled with denial, born of the fear of Jesus's teachings.

"I like that," says Marianne of the course premise. "I take comfort in that. It means that all the love, all the trust we feel and all the beneficience and beauty are real, and all the rest is a dream we're having that we made."

The course teaches we are all one, and the symbol of oneness is Christ. Its aim, therefore, is to heal the separation ego created. Ultimate enlightenment, therefore, is attained by seeing the world through the eyes of Christ, or the oneself. In the course, the concept of "miracle" is not an act of divine intervention beyond natural law, but a metaphor for correcting an individual's false thinking. A "miracle," then, is a radical shift in perception that transforms the fear rooted in that illusory world into love, the holistic viewpoint of the Holy Spirit. Rejecting the illusion of our separateness and accepting our oneness allows us to relinquish hatred and replace it with forgiveness. We undo our guilt at our own massive attack on God by practicing Jesus' example of forgiveness, of others and ourselves. Forgiveness is at the core of the course, and nonjudgment is the key.

The course's true message of the atonement is "the undoing of guilt through forgiveness," says the newsletter, forgiveness for something that *seemed* to happen in this world of illusion and therefore did not *actually* happen.

"*A Course in Miracles'* definition of forgiveness is not the traditional definition of the term," Marianne translates. "Ordinarily, forgiveness is something you do when somebody has been a jerk, but now you are 'spiritual,' so you forgive them. *A Course in Miracles* calls that mere judgment, an arrogant perception. Real forgiveness is recognizing that only love in people is real, that's the crux of the course."

If this world is illusory, and no human event—including Jesus' suffering on the cross—is real, you forgive your brother for what he has *not* done. In other words, because only love is real, there is nothing to forgive. Nothing has been done to you; it's all something that you did to yourself. The miracle is achieved when you are able to shift from the ego-mind, which thinks in terms of attack, blame, and hatred, to that of the Holy Spirit, which views all with only love. God's unconditional love is extended to us, and through us to others. If we practice forgiveness, Jesus did not die on the cross in vain. We are living according to the same principles of forgiveness that He demonstrated. The more we do what He says, the more we will understand what He taught and the closer we will come to Him.

The principles of the course are summarized in fifty brief statements in the text's first chapter, beginning with: "There is no order of difficulty in miracles. One is not harder or bigger than another. They are all the same. All expressions of love are maximal."

Though Marianne and other course interpreters have been criticized for focusing overly on relationships, the course itself emphasizes the importance of relationships. *A Course in Miracles* is not about withdrawing in monkish fashion from the world in order to contemplate God's grandeur. "Relationships are the temple of the Holy Spirit," teaches the course. Only two types of relationships exist between people: "special" relationships, such as those most of us have with our lovers, and "holy" relationships, the kind most of us *should* have with our lovers, and with everyone else. The fearful "ego-mind" directs us to "special" relationships, which by their very nature separate one from the rest of humanity and are usually based on hidden bargains. In a holy relationship, one does not single out another as special or try to get something from someone else simply because they are sleeping together. In the "holy" relationship, the kind ideally we would share with all our brothers and sisters, people simply love others as they are, and in turn are open to being loved for themselves alone. That is because each of us is the same, a son of the Holy Spirit.

"Whenever you meet anyone," the course says, "remember it is a holy encounter. As you see him, you will see yourself. As you treat him, you will treat yourself. Never forget this, for in him you will find yourself or lose yourself."

Of course, the foremost barrier to evolvement beyond ego-understanding is the special relationship. The course was given to us by Jesus, who spoke of undoing that specialness. If the message is threatening, its author must be as well. Therefore, Jesus "remains the greatest symbol of the ego's love and hate," says Wapnick, "a special relationship that needs to be worked through *with* him, so it can be forgiven. Only then would it be possible for students of the course to know that *they* are truly forgiven."

It is interesting to note here that as Marianne became more and more identified as a symbol of the course, she also began to experience similarly confused projections of love and hate from some of her followers.

Course students "are often tempted to speak only about love and joining, as understood through the lens of their specialness," Wapnick notes in the newsletter, but the student's focus shouldn't be on love per se, he says.

> "We should place our efforts in looking with Jesus at our desire to keep separate from God and His son, for this desire is what prevents us from knowing we are truly joined as one Son with the Source of Love.
>
> It is not love that is the goal of *A Course in Miracles*, but the forgiveness of the specialness we cherish and hold dear *because* we made it to exclude love. We must first experience the peace of forgiveness before we could remember the Love of God.

Followers of established religions question the validity of *A Course in Miracles* as compared to another "scribed" work, the bible. "The God of the Bible is really like a glorified ego," explains Kenneth Wapnick. "He has his good days and bad days; He loves, but it's always with a hitch. If you don't do what He wants, He kills you. He's very much into sacrifice, concerned with idolatry, and He kills His enemies. At the same time, He's loving and forgiving. He's like anybody else, and, obviously, that's the ego part. The position the course would take on the Bible, although it never specifically said this, would be consistent with everything else it's said, that the Bible is a mixed bag. It has inspired elements, and it has ego elements. It often reflects the thought system of the ego, and that is one of the major purposes of the course: to set the record straight. God is not a God of specialness, he's not a God of sacrifice. He doesn't want His children to sacrifice, and He didn't sacrifice His son, Jesus. As matter of fact, we're all part of this sonship. Love doesn't sacrifice, love doesn't kill, love doesn't demand. Love simply accepts. Also, in the Old and New Testaments, God created the world and is very much involved in it and in people's behaviors. In fact, the Ten Commandments are geared very much toward what people do: Thou shalt not do this, that, or the other thing. The God of the course is not involved with behavior at all. The focus of the course is not to change your behavior, but to change your thinking. The emphasis is totally different."

Those who are most critical and know least about *A Course in Miracles* charge that it is just the start of another cult. While people can become obsessive about the course, they receive no encouragement from any organization, because other than the Foundation for Inner Peace, which publishes the course, and the Foundation for *A Course in Miracles*, which oversees its translations, there is no organization. Although informal study groups spring up here and there, and people have been on occasion moved to lecture on course principles, *A Course in Miracles* is basically a self-study program. Course students are not encouraged to withdraw from existing contacts, to place management of their money or affairs in the hands of a guru, to submit to discipline, or any of the other familiar accoutrements of abusive cult practice.

While simply plowing through the course text can be difficult, the workbook that accompanies the text can make the principles of the course much more accessible and applicable to students' daily lives. By practicing the 360 spiritual lessons of the workbook —one for every day of the year—the principles laid out in the text take on real meaning. Lesson 1, for example, prepares the student to separate from his attachment to the illusion of the world by teaching, "Nothing I see in this room [on this street, from this window, in this place] means anything." Lesson 31 furthers that detachment from ego-based fear by teaching that "I am not the victim of the world I see." Students are recommended to engage in three to five minutes of "practice" of each lesson in the morning and at night. The student spends time looking out at the world while repeating the day's concept silently, then closing his eyes to apply the same idea to his inner world. The workbook exercises allow a student of the course to train his mind in changes of perceptions; they are essentially guidelines to the creation of miracles.

An important key to understanding the course is that unlike other spiritual disciplines that teach that the world as we know it is *maya*, or illusion, the course does not hint of any contempt for worldly experience. This world is our classroom, and each experience is our teacher. Ideally, we grasp the lesson to be learned in each tribulation or problem. In fact, the point is not finding a solution to each problem, but to grow in spiritual strength as we find those solutions.

How does one span the chasm from a nearly chronic condition of fear-based behavior to loving oneself and one's fellow man unconditionally, all the time? One can only try, through prayer and service to others.

Many course students fall into a trap of self-blame because they feel they cannot avoid judgment and cannot achieve complete forgiveness and unconditional love. But the course teaches that a willing intention is enough. Says Pat Buckley:

> I'll never forget the first time I did the lesson book. I had an office on Park Avenue at the time, and my lesson for the day was "I will not judge anyone." So I walked down Park Avenue vowing I wouldn't judge anyone. I saw a woman and thought, "Isn't that a nice outfit!" And then I thought, "Oh my God, that's a judgment." Because that's a posi-

tive, which means there's a negative. But Ken Wapnick says "Don't make the error real." And Marianne has a different way of saying it. People can get confused with that because we function on two levels. We function on "I am a body; I can't deny it," but, at the same time, we function on a metaphysical, quantum type of approach, "Okay, this is an illusion but I'm going to use it as my classroom. I'm not going to use it as my attack-defense, victimization thing. I'm going to change my mind. It's my choice to have my guide be the Holy Spirit or Jesus, or whatever you want to call it." It doesn't matter, words are secondary. If I'm too stuck in the guilt or fear, that's going to be my ego trip. Whenever I feel that, I have to take responsibility and say, "Okay, this is silly. I'm going to look at it with a loving presence whom I happen to call Jesus." I say "Jesus, help me see this differently." Sometimes just "help" is a very good prayer.

"The process of cause and effect is the basic law of human consciousness," says Marianne. "If we so choose, however, we can change our thoughts, then experience changes accordingly. *A Course in Miracles* says love is real because it is God, and God is all that exists. 'What is all-encompassing can have no opposite.' So anything that is not loving is actually an illusion."

"You can do much on behalf of your own healing

and that of others," the course teaches, "if, in a situation calling for Help, you think of it this way:

> I am here only to be truly helpful.
> I am here to represent Him who sent me.
> I do not have to worry about what to say or what to do, because He Who sent me will direct me.
> I am content to be wherever He wishes, knowing He goes there with me.
> I will be healed as I let Him teach me to heal.

"*A Course in Miracles* says that these ideas become true for you as you *do* them," Marianne explains. You invoke what it is you want to see, consciously. You see, some people think that faith in God is separate from faith in people. So, if you don't have faith in people, your faith in God will not seem justified. Put your faith in people, à la Pollyanna, and then invoke this faith in people that allows you to see the *love* in people rather than just the fear. And your faith is justified because you yourself played your part. When you see your faith justified, what you are really seeing reflected back is that you decided to do your bit today. If you do your bit today, you will feel more hopeful. Everybody's thinking that 'I'll be more faithful if I see something outside myself.' There is nothing outside ourselves.

"That is the ultimate knowledge," she continues, "that there is nothing outside yourself. One of the radical aspects of *A Course in Miracles* is that there is no relationship with the Father outside the relationship with the Son. So you can't have faith in God without the faith that you have in His Son, because that is where He *is*.

"So you have faith in the goodness in people. It's all choice. I choose to have faith in people, then it's my way of casting my vote for a world which reflects back that I was right. No matter what—you are going to be right! *A Course in Miracles* says that projection makes perception. The course says that you decide what you want to see and then you see it. But it happens so quickly that oftentimes we don't see it take place."

As lofty and unattainable as some course principles may appear, the course does teach that there is "no order of miracles." The slightest shift in thought and behavior qualifies. At an early part of her studies in the course, Judith Skutch asked Bill Thetford, "How can you tell if you're really getting it; if you're really going along, absorbing this and it's working in you?"

"Well dearie," he answered. "You could do this. Ask yourself, 'How long do I hold a grievance?' "

"I was pretty good at doing that, and I realized that I held it much less time," says Skutch. "If my husband doesn't do exactly what I want him to do or if I'm waiting for someone to call me back, I realize it just blows over now. If I start to get excited, I laugh, which doesn't mean 'deny,' it means 'look at and make a choice.' It's a conscious choice. My mother had a friend quite a few years ago whose husband died 'too early,' as she thought. They were very, very close—it was really quite a remarkable marriage—

and she went to pieces. She grieved and grieved and grieved. She wouldn't go out with anyone; her children found her to be a dried-up old prune. One day my mother went over to visit her and she said, 'You know Doris, if you want to, you can be happy. I know you had a wonderful marriage with Dave and you just deeply regret that he's not here anymore, but that happens to a lot of people. After a time, you start to heal, and you remember him with love, but you also pay attention to other people who love you. You can have happiness from that.' But Doris said, 'I will *not* be happy!' A very clear, beautiful statement," Skutch comments. "She recognized that it was a choice: 'I will *not!*' She died not happy."

After she had been practicing the course for nine years, Marianne gave a lecture on the nature of fear, which offered a beautifully lucid example drawn from her own life of the way in which the course can transform one's perception, and, parenthetically, the amazingly baroque defenses of a terrified ego.

"There are so many areas of my life where I used to experience major fear and no longer do," she opened. "I'm not saying I don't have moments of them, but major areas of my life have been largely healed. My ego used to be this huge, gray monster. Now it's this little black poisonous insect. The huge gray monster used to have the run in my life; the insect can't cover a lot of ground, but, boy, when it's there, it's like poison." Marianne then went on to describe a fear of flying that had recently overtaken her, and her futile attempts to overcome it. Finally, a friend described Kenneth Wapnick's response to a rock climber who sometimes experienced fear. "What you really need to ask yourself after you get a good psychotherapist to help you figure out why you would want to climb rocks," Wapnick said, "is who have you not forgiven?"

At first, Marianne said, she could not see a connection between her fear of flying and a need to forgive someone. "It seemed to me that my ego was working more on a control thing," she said. 'How dare I be in a situation where I'm not the driver?' I could recognize my own weaknesses as a possible source of my fear. But every time I picked up the course, I would read something like, 'The fear of God results as surely from the lesson that His Son is guilty, as God's love must be remembered when He learns his innocence. For hate must father fear and look upon its father as itself. How wrong are you who fail to hear the call that echoes past each seeming call to death, that sings behind each murderous attack and pleads that love restore the dying world. You do not understand who calls to you beyond each form of hate, each call to war. Yet you will recognize Him as you give Him answer in the language that He calls. He will appear when you answer Him and you will know in Him that God is love.'

"What the course is saying there," Marianne said in another brilliantly succinct and down-to-earth interpretation, "is 'Don't kid yourself.' It doesn't say behind your fear is a need to control. It says behind your fear is a belief that someone is guilty. So I started to think about my own thoughts. So often I've said to people, if you have a problem about money, it's not a problem about money, it's the fact that you feel you don't deserve money. There's always some area where you think 'I'm too guilty, I don't deserve it.' It seemed to me I'd gotten to the point where I know I deserve money, I know I deserve a man, I just don't think I deserve to live! And that is exactly what was happening. Sometimes I would be on an airplane and I would think, 'Why am I going?' Then I would feel a voice answering, 'I'm sending you out to save the world.' 'Well, I know that's my ego,' I would think, 'that can't be God talking because that sounds awfully grandiose.' Then I would get back, 'Hey, wait a minute. I didn't say only you. I didn't say you were special. It's the same answer I would tell anybody. It just happens to be everybody's assignment. That's what you don't want to accept. But you do deserve something as magnificent as hanging around in order to do a glorious task. On some level you just don't think you deserve it.' So I thought to myself, 'Well, wait a minute. If you're going to say to me, "All you have to do is love yourself and really believe you deserve to be here, that you are not guilty," then all you have to do is just forgive yourself.' The statement of forgiveness is that all the love that has ever occurred is real, and that everything else is just an hallucination. One of the exercises early on in the workbook is, 'God did not create such and such, therefore it does not exist.' One of the actual suggestions given in the exercise is, 'God did not create that airline disaster; therefore, it does not exist.' This was a hard one for me because it was my own particular little forming phobia. What I was reminded of—and this is so interesting to me, we talk about this all the time, but there are ways for me in which it doesn't always hit home—whenever you see something, you're just seeing a little edge, the tip of the iceberg of someone's experience."

CHAPTER SIX

L.A. WOMAN

Marianne had emerged from her twenties "wanting, from the depths of my being, to be a good woman," she says. "We do not have, in this generation, a base of consciousness about service and devotion and reverence. The world is dominated by a thought system of selfishness. But I really want to devote the rest of my life to helping people. Suffering gives you X-ray vision into other people's suffering."

It was 1983, Marianne was thirty-one years old, but her admirable intentions had yet to coalesce into any plan of action. Building a career simply from being "a good woman" was an unlikely notion at best. So Marianne headed west, for reasons that she's vague about even now. "I had one thousand dollars," she says. "I knew one person, Sarah McMullen, with whom I'd been a cheerleader in junior high school, and I didn't have a job.

Before long she was working part-time at the

Philosophical Research Society, once a supplier of books for her store, typing, filing, and handling office chores.

Kent Black, who worked at the society, told the *Los Angeles Times* that he remembers "a brassy, sassy Texas woman climbing out of a big desert cruiser in front of the society's office. She was wearing cowboy boots and her trunk was filled with *A Course in Miracles.* I thought she had a lot of chutzpah. She just elbowed her way in."

An intriguing image, but in fact Marianne carried with her only a single copy of *A Course in Miracles,* she was driving her mother's silver Oldsmobile, and she felt anything but "brassy and sassy." "I just asked for a job," Marianne recalls. "When I gave my résumé to Pat Ervin, who was then vice-president, she noticed I had worked for the Foundation for Inner Peace, and she said, 'I've been looking for someone to give lectures on the course.' I was so excited. She asked if I had ever lectured on it, and I told her I used to lead groups in my store. By that time I had been a course student for five years. So I worked part-time and I came home every day to read, read, read. I read that thing in a way I never had before in order to prepare for my first lecture. The course says that to call yourself a teacher of God, make sure you have finished the workbook."

Before Marianne gave her first introductory talk on *A Course in Miracles,* she papered the town with flyers, and was rewarded by an audience of seventy-five. "I worked so hard to prepare that talk," she recalls. "Pat Ervin called me that day and said, 'That was very good. Would you like to do it every Saturday for a year?' That was how my career started. Then I started lecturing on Tuesdays."

In the beginning, the crowds were smaller but faithful. "About thirty people would come," Marianne recalls, "and I'd bring ginger ale for everybody. The only difference between then and now—I wore bigger earrings." Eventually Marianne outgrew the Philosophical Research Society. "They didn't like that too many people started coming and that I prayed," Marianne says with a smile. "Pat Ervin thought that was wrong. But she gave me my career."

Lynda Obst was already a successful Hollywood film producer, working at the Geffen Company when Marianne moved to California and paid a visit to her former roommate:

I think in the beginning I was wondering if she expected me to do something for her. When you first start getting successful, you worry "Omigod, are you supposed to get the person a job?" So I wasn't as open to what she was going through as I would be now if I met her. She was a little bit lost, and I guess I could have helped her more than I did. But I didn't know what that meant beyond getting her a job, and she didn't seem to want one. She was working at the Philosophical Research Society, which didn't make sense

to me. I didn't get the picture. And I was sort
of a rolling stone, gathering not a lot of moss
at that time in my own life, going through
changes in my own marriage.

"I never had any idea that I was going to be doing
this," says Marianne. "Some of the places in my life
where I've been totally naive have been the places
where I've been most blessed. I had major purity
when I began because I had no idea lectures were
given to a lot of people, that you could make a living
doing it, and you could write books. I used to bring
in maybe thirty dollars a month and I supported
myself as a temporary secretary for two years."

In 1985 Marianne met David Kessler, who is now
the president of the board of the Los Angeles Center
for Living. At the time, he owned a nursing service
and home health-care agency specializing in serving
people with AIDS and hospice care. He was also
running several AIDS support groups. A mutual
friend of Williamson's and Kessler's approached him
to ask if Marianne could use his apartment for her
Monday night prayer meeting since he was running
a support group on that night at a different location.
Kessler agreed. "I'd come home from my support
group," he recalls. "Marianne would finish her
group, and we got to know each other by chatting
after our groups."

Back home in Houston, Marianne's parents struggled to understand their youngest child. In 1984
Sam was honored at a roast to benefit the Statue of

Liberty/Ellis Island Foundation. In an interview with the *Houston Post*, he referred to Marianne as "a nightclub singer in California and into the occult. But she has a good brain and I tried to get her to go to law school."

Today, after having listened to many of her lectures, he is more supportive. "The words seem different," he says, "but we really speak the same language."

"She associates it with the Golden Rule," Sophie Ann explained to *Vanity Fair*. "I used to kid her about being like Aimee Semple McPherson, but Marianne says, 'Jesus and the Holy Spirit—Mother, they're just words for goodness. I am not spouting Christianity.'" Then a hint of tenacious disappointment peeps through. "If I'd been asked what I would have preferred for her to have done, I would have said, 'Be a lawyer.' I think she would have been a terrific lawyer. But this brings her happiness."

Marianne continued to attend Jewish High Holy Day services "to make my mother happy."

Television actress Melanie Chartoff met Marianne during that first year of lecturing. Trapped in a destructive relationship, Chartoff had begun studying the course at a friend's suggestion. "I was absolutely entranced by it because it was exactly what I needed to be doing at that particular time," she says. That same friend also recommended that Melanie get in touch with a woman who was holding Sunday discussion groups on the course and lived on Hayward Street in the same West Hollywood neighborhood. One Sunday, Melanie walked three blocks, knocked on Marianne's door, and "was greeted by this bare-foot, no makeup, short-haired, cutie pie." Approximately ten people were sitting around her living room. "She navigated the discussion in a very glib, articulate way, which I immediately related to," Chartoff recalls. "We were very interested in each other; we were both lapsed Jewesses with a gift for gab. I brought another actress, Betty Buckley, also from Texas, to meet Marianne and join this discussion group. We palled around a little bit, but we never got terribly close because our businesses were in different areas." Chartoff recalls going to Marianne's exercise class. "We worked out at the Voight" —a West Hollywood exercise salon—"once; she dragged me there. It wasn't for me, it was too serious. But I was extremely impressed with Marianne's stamina, self-discipline, and her physical strength. She's in great shape and can work really hard, as was evidenced by the hour and a half workout; she went the whole distance."

The women also enjoyed "flexing their intellects within a spiritual motif," and Chartoff recalls being "terribly impressed at how this little cutie pie, who looked like a little girl, was able to field a lot of the confusion and rage evidenced by the people in the room."

A man "who had a very advanced case of AIDS was pleading for understanding" during one session, Chartoff recalls. "Marianne dealt with him a very eloquent, simple way. She had no fear of anyone's rage. She seemed to be able to dismantle it and look at it quite objectively. One morning, Betty was railing at God about the confusion He has foisted on mankind about sex and spirit and love and differences between them. She was so angry at God, she was really chewing Him out. Marianne blithely observed this and was able to sum it up, deflect a lot of the anger, and rechannel it into a way of thinking. I was terribly impressed with her."

Marianne and Melanie had a few "shy lunches" together, and then Melanie did seek out Marianne's counsel when "I was going nuts about this guy I was obsessed with. I had a session with her in which she was extremely generous. She talked to me a good deal from the context of the *Course in Miracles*," Chartoff says, noting that "at a later lunch we were able to share that we both had this obsessive unavailable-men syndrome common to a lot of complicated women."

At a point when Chartoff was struggling in her acting career, she remembers visiting Marianne and her roommate at the time, actress Laura Dern. "I hadn't worked for a few years and I went to see her because I was getting so addicted to the idea of not working, that I was probably going to make it not happen," Chartoff says. "I looked at Laura, who was brought up in the biz with both parents successful actors." Bruce Dern and Diane Ladd. "In her mind, there was no question she would be a film actress. There was none of that addictive quality about it. Marianne said to me, 'I wish that for you, that you believe you're an actress, you'll be working, and there's nothing to get "Omigod, it will never happen!" about.' "

In 1984 June Smith, Marianne's high school teacher, was in Los Angeles with friends for the Olympics. Marianne was still lecturing for the society. "I heard her speak there," Smith recalls. "I remember specifically what she said, 'Jesus is just the same as we are, except what Jesus has, he has completely down to the last subatomic part of him. We only have it in one subatomic part of us.' It told me that there might be something else, but it wasn't just hearing her lecture. We spent the day together and we talked a lot. She told me what was happening in her life, and we really connected again. I realized how important the course was to her and how much she had learned and grown from it. When I learned that the *Course in Miracles* teaches that God did not create this world, I thought, 'Maybe this is something I can deal with.' I never wanted any part of a system in which whatever kind of God created this world, because who needs it? Unfortunately, we seem to need the ego that created it too. I'm very grateful for that connection in L.A."

. Marianne's prayer groups were becoming less discussion and more lecture on her part on subjects related to the *Course in Miracles.* She now lectured regularly at two churches: at the Unitarian Church in Santa Monica on Sunday evenings, and on Franklin Avenue in West Hollywood on Saturday mornings. "By the time I got out there to see her in 1984," says Tama Walker, "she had a big church and was lecturing to fifty to seventy-five people."

Among Marianne's most enthusiastic early supporters were the gay community, particularly those affected directly by the AIDS crisis. Shunned by traditional religion and social services, they embraced Marianne and her message of loving nonjudgment, and as her lecture audience grew, requests were made for private counseling.

"I met Marianne shortly after she first started lecturing in Los Angeles," says Dick de Vogeleare, who later became the third director for the L.A. Center for Living. "It was in the Los Feliz area, and I had originally been doing a *Course in Miracles* study group in Hollywood. I heard she had a large gay following in Silver Lake. 'That sounds perfect for me,' I thought. I was extremely enamored, and I began following her around everywhere. She moved into Hollywood, and I became more and more involved; I started doing the music for her lectures around Christmastime. One thing led to another. Projects came up. We began serving the homeless dinners around holiday times, and I started to take charge of those. The Center for Living was created. I was involved with that and fund-raising projects. I was always around."

When de Vogeleare discovered Marianne was doing private counseling, "I liked her so much that when various issues came up in my own life, I would call her, make an appointment, and we would sit. She's a very, very insightful woman; she's got gifts when it comes to that. We would have a session for about an hour, come to some conclusion, and we would pray all the time over the problem. The next day or several days later, she'd call me at the office and ask, 'How's everything?' She showed a real personal interest in me."

By now Marianne had the course down cold, but she added her own spin, much as a jazz musician improvises on the classics. Drawing on a range of other theosophies and philosophies, psychology, metaphysics and pop culture, and using the performance skills she'd developed during her cabaret years, Marianne made the course sing.

Her particular skill, according to former boyfriend Jeff Olmsted, was in making "spiritual matters relevant to her own generation—something that young, liberal urban professionals can relate to."

The key to Marianne's extraordinary gift for bringing the principles of the course to life and connecting so compellingly with her audience certainly had to do with her articulateness and warmth as a speaker. But even more significant, Marianne Williamson was willing to share open and honest appraisals of her experiences with the audience—not to produce, as she terms it, "a Marianne Williamson Show," but to use those anecdotes as instructive examples. Marianne's audience could identify readily with this pretty, intelligent, wisecracking woman who seemed to have it together—and in many ways did—but who nonetheless struggled with the very same issues they did.

No one else so successfully combined the sophisticated spiritual concepts of the course with such down-to-earth practical issues as weight problems, roommate difficulties, trouble on the job, and the heartbreak of romance.

Howard Rosenman, a Los Angeles-based film producer, told *Vanity Fair:*

> The first time I went to see her it was like the Liberty Bell fell on my head. Here was this gorgeous Jewish chick who obviously came from a sophisticated, neurotic Texas Jewish background, talking in the argot of my generation, bringing together strands of sociology, politics, anthropology, history, science, and the Bible. The community she's addressing is a group that partied and drugged and sexualized through the sixties and seventies, and here comes this woman who looks like one of us, who you know could have been at Studio 54 or dancing at Fire Island Pines with a tambourine on her hip—and yet she's talking like Jesus Christ. She's talking about the most fundamental precepts. She's talking about the Golden Rule.

Even when "playing to [concerns] of her generation," the author of that *Vanity Fair* piece commented, she would keep the discussion within spiritual-religious dimensions through references to the Holy Spirit and Jesus. "All that Christ is is the unconditionally loving essence of every person," she would repeat. While Marianne made references to a dizzyingly wide-ranging collection of subjects and synthesized them to her points, she always was on guard to deflect her audience's tendency to regard her as the source. More often than not, her remarks would be prefaced by the phrase, "The *Course in Miracles* says . . ."

Melanie Chartoff comments:

I think her work in the course is extremely pure. I don't think her persona taints the actual work; just listen to her tapes. I think it's her physicality that's very arresting and compelling and can be distracting. I remember she had me over to her apartment in 1985 or 1986 to see her videotape because she was planning a pilot for a network show. She already had this Channel 3 program on public access TV, an amateur job. There were four or five of us over on a Saturday night to see a tape of the public access show, and she was a nervous wreck, terrified of what I'd think. I guess she was like I was when I first saw myself on television. Everything looked horrible and I could only see my faults. I was tearing myself apart—"Why did I do *that*?" She was sitting there, slaughtering herself the same way, going "No, no!" She kept looking down and saying "I do it much better now!" She was really anxious about how she was coming across. It was so surprising because she looked absolutely adorable on television, completely herself, completely natural. She was very self-critical, but it was wonderful because she was human. The ambition she was letting me see

was raw. She's one of the most giving, generous souls I've ever met, and she really goes
for it without a net. I think she didn't like her
naturalness; she didn't like the essence of
herself, and that kind of disturbed me because I thought the wonderful contrast of
her barefoot, short-haired, no makeup innocence with the brilliance and wit coming out
of her mouth was so wonderful.

Shauna Hoffman and her partner produced two
tapes that year, an introduction to the course and
another on relationships, that until recently were
available in New Age bookstores across the country.
Like virtually everyone who was gathering around
Williamson, Hoffman had been inspired by attending a lecture. Says Hoffman, who a few years later
was married in a ceremony officiated by Williamson:

She used to speak very, very quickly. It
was one thought after the other after the
other. Many people say "I stop it, rewind and
go back and listen to that again because she
said it so fast and I wanted to get what she
said." She's learned so much as far as
speaking more clearly and making her point
more clearly. That has changed, as has her
volume level. She also used to talk very
loudly. Now she's much more peaceful,
much more centered. But one thing that was
amazing about watching the old tapes was
that it was so obviously being given to her,

especially because it was coming that fast. There was not a moment to think. It was just one idea after another after another. One of the tapes records her lecture completely as it was—boom, boom, boom. It was lecture, followed by question and answer. During the shoot of the relationship tape, our close-up camera on Marianne went down. So we wrote out the audience's questions, let them go, and then fed Marianne the questions while we did close-ups on her so that we would have a choice on the answers when she was in a close-up. Of course, the answers were similar, but they weren't exactly the same. She doesn't rattle off the same exact thing; she's inspired differently at every moment. But she was unbelievably unshaken by the situation. She's an incredible professional.

"I began to feel that her mystique was growing," Melanie Chartoff says. "Although she constantly deflected to her audience, saying 'I am not the *Course in Miracles*, I'm just reading it, and anybody can figure this stuff out,' she became, I felt, the lazy man's way to get the precepts of the course. It wasn't my fix.

"I began to feel that Marianne's personality was so compelling and captivating that it was keeping me from doing the work I needed to do on the book alone. For me the *Course in Miracles* is an extremely personal journey and I like to do it in my own time frame. Sometimes I like to linger on one lesson for a month. It's very intellectual and brilliant. It uses the ego to dismantle the ego. I find it difficult to believe that a human being could have written it, could be that clear on neurosis, anxiety. I was so impressed with it."

Chartoff also began to feel the lectures had become "a social gathering for the spiritually afflicted," not her cup of tea but nonetheless "a wonderful thing."

"Marianne's image began to grow more glamorous," Chartoff also notes. "She began investing in her beauty; she has a very profound beauty, and she was working it as one has to work it in this particular town."

In her book, Marianne recounts a past romance with an Italian man who initially discomforted her by appearing for their dates dressed in a suit and overcoat. Ultimately, she realized that "his dressing up was a way to please me, a way of communicating how much he cared."

Although Marianne speaks often of the detrimental effects created by the advertising industry's efforts to convince women that their desirability is determined by their physical appeal, she had come to view makeup and fashion as something other than mere narcissistic display. "Their point is not to seduce another person, but to add light to the world in the form of beauty and pleasure," she writes in her book. "The meaning in things is how much we use them to contribute happiness to the world. Clothes and other personal effects are no different than any other art form. If we perceive them lovingly, they can lift the vibrations and increase the energy in the world around us."

In actuality Marianne had always worn makeup when she lectured. Part of Marianne's new image was due to the ministrations of Arthur Luna, a hairdresser who was a course student and a Williamson lecture fan. One night he walked up to her after a lecture and said, "I really want to do your hair, I'd love for you to be my client."' Luna explains: "When I'd go see her lecture, I would think, 'God, I'd really love to cut her hair, make her hair look really good.' I think it was permed at the time."

Marianne took Luna up on his offer and came into the Beverly Hills salon where he worked. "She was very open," Luna says, "and we started gradually changing her look and getting her into a more one-length, chic look, as opposed to light and airy. Her hair was great for the time because it was the early eighties and that was the style. I just took her through the styles, and she's really into it because she likes looking good.

"We became friends, and every time she needed her hair done for something, I'd go over to her house. It was a way to know her without having to see her as the lecturer, Marianne Williamson, and also of entering her private space. She was just wonderful; I loved talking to her. She was a crack-up. There's a person behind there who lives just as we do, deals with things just like you do. And you think, 'Omigod, she has the same problem I do!' I admired her because she had a normal life and also an insight that most people don't have. The two combined are great. I'd see her life and how great she is and how much fun and how fashionable. To this day I still call her up and say, 'What's the deal? Are you doing something? Let me do your hair for you.' "

Marianne was receiving a great deal of help in her personal life with the course, but she still felt a need for psychological counseling. When she and Melanie Chartoff had lunch one day, they discovered they had begun psychotherapy the same month. As they discussed how the course and psychotherapy work together, Chartoff realized that Marianne's psychotherapist had treated a close friend of hers who had since died. "I didn't think she did a great job with my friend," says Chartoff, "and I was stricken. I sort of said, 'Oh, no! Not her! I'm anxious about her for you.' But I was also aware that Marianne is incredibly strong and incredibly bright, and certainly wouldn't be any therapist's victim, because it's an area where she plays the game very, very well. She knows the mind very, very well."

After that lunch, the two women drifted apart, and, at the same time, Chartoff moved from *A Course in Miracles* to other, "more social, universal, less conceptual forms of spiritualism."

Jaquel Prier and Marianne formed a friendship when Jaquel was dating one of Marianne's best friends. Jaquel attended Marianne's lectures before moving to Colorado in 1987, where she booked seminars for her friend. When Jaquel's fourteen-year-old daughter was severely brain-damaged in a car accident, "the first person I called was Marianne at two A.M. We got on a prayer line and she came to Colorado," Jaquel recalls. "My daughter woke from a month-long coma on Easter. We had to teach her how to swallow, talk, breathe, think—everything— all over again. Her face was smashed. She was a total vegetable. I was really into positive thinking and we did a lot of prayer work. Marianne, another girl, and I would sit around and pray. This kid is up and walking today, and you'd never know anything was wrong. Even the doctors say they have no ex- planation. The surgeon had said she had double brain injury and there was no way that she should even be up walking, but she's starting college next year. The doctor used to see her even after she healed, just because he just couldn't understand it. She was in the accident in March, and I took her out of the hospital in a walker on June tenth.

"Marianne kept me very centered," Jaquel says. "She would pray with me every night if I needed it. Her prayer was the clinching factor that helped me keep my sanity, having one person on the planet to call up and say, 'I need help!' Instead of giving me information or chitchat, she would say, 'Let's pray.' That was the entire conversation, 'Let's pray.' She'd sit down with Andie and pray with her even though she wasn't conscious. Marianne did what needed to be done to the soul, and the doctors did what needed to be done on the body."

Inspired by her example of devoted friendship, a group of like-minded people was growing around Marianne, more of an extended family than mere

friends. And Marianne's ministry was expanding beyond what a single person could handle.

Susan Phelan recalls a friend telling her one day
about Marianne's introductory lecture at the Beverly Theater in Beverly Hills. Phelan, who was already a student of the course, resisted attending
because she couldn't imagine what anyone could
possibly tell her about the course that she didn't
already know. But she went, kicking and screaming. "Marianne got on the stage without saying a
word," Phelan recalls, "and I was dissolved in tears
by her presence. It was really an amazing moment.
Then, of course, her lecture was wonderful, and I
started going to the Saturday morning lectures on a
regular basis. At that time she was giving prayer
groups in her home where maybe ten or fifteen people would attend. Then just through attending the
lectures, I became friendly with her and ultimately
ended up as her personal assistant beginning in
1985."

Phelan had worked in human services and as a
costumer in the film industry. In between jobs in the
film business at the time, she viewed Marianne's request as a "perfect opportunity for me. I felt very
honored and excited to work closely with her, and it
was an amazing learning experience."

Her work duties covered everything from personal
caretaking, such as taking in Marianne's dry clean-
ing, helping with the production and organization of
the audio tapes that were just beginning to be made
and distributed, general office work such as setting
appointments and administering to her business af-

fairs, even counseling people on the telephone if Marianne wasn't available. "It was a labor of love," Phelan says today. "Her ministry was just becoming very attractive to people, and people were taking notice of the course. But it was still very much an underground, esoteric study. It's only been in the last three years that it really mushroomed."

Though a few recent articles on Marianne have highlighted reports of her supposedly ungovernable temper, Phelan views the matter differently:

> What I experienced from Marianne was an incredible level of honesty and an equally amazing level of intimacy she allowed into her life. Because I worked out of her second bedroom, I was there with her from morning to night and I saw every aspect of Marianne, in terms of who she is as a human being. Not the teacher, although I was certainly aware of the teacher personality, but the personality of the human being, which is why, some eight years later, I continue to call her my dearest friend, somebody whom I love very deeply, who has also been a powerful teacher in my life.
>
> That's not to say that she doesn't have a personality. She runs the full gamut. I think that "passion" is probably the word that best characterizes her. Also "honesty," "authenticity." What you see with Marianne is what you get. The large part of what is so wonderful about her is that she doesn't hold back.

She tells you her life; she's lived it all, and she freely tells you and draws upon her life for her object lessons as they relate to the *Course in Miracles*. It's not like you're going to some guru who's pretending he's never lived a life or he never got angry or never had sex. That is not who Marianne is.

If I ever felt afraid or in awe of her myself, it was my problem. The times that I found the courage within me to say the truth about something, she was so grateful. I have found that by just sticking to your guns, she respects you a whole lot more. There was one time we were talking about a relationship that had ended for her, and she wasn't understanding. She had a need to communicate with this person and was in a turmoil about it. I took a risk and told her the truth, how I observed the situation. Not only was she extremely grateful, she referenced my comment in a lecture. When people are afraid to say the truth to Marianne and are yes-sayers to her, she views that as a disservice. This is a woman who is extremely bright and intuitive, and she knows when people aren't being straight with her. That's why she will act frustrated. She knows there's something else to be said here and they're not saying it. Not to say that it isn't a shared responsibility too, it obviously is. But I know when I was coming from that place of feeling little and frightened and didn't want

Marianne Williamson, pictured here with older siblings Jane and Peter, was born into a middle-class Jewish family and grew up in Houston, Texas.
(From the collection of Marianne Williamson)

Although she hated Sunday school, those close to Marianne say that she was very religious as a child. At bedtime she would often chastise her mother: "Go away Mommy, I'm talking to God."
(From the collection of Marianne Williamson)

Among Williamson's followers are some of Hollywood's brightest stars, including Elizabeth Taylor and new husband Larry Fortensky. Marianne officiated at their October 6, 1991 wedding, which was held at the ranch of singer Michael Jackson. *(Paul Pelletieri/courtesy of the Ford Group)*

Marianne Williamson with *(left to right)* Shirley MacLaine, Leslie Ann Warren and David Kessler at a July 1991 fundraiser for the Los Angeles Center for Living. The event raised $55,000 for the charity. *(From the collection of David Kessler)*

Marianne Williamson is the founder of the Los Angeles free home delivery service, Project Angel Food. Many Hollywood luminaries, including Shirley MacLaine *(pictured here)*, have become involved in the project.
(Nancy Rosenquist/from the collection of Marianne Williamson)

Marianne's daughter, India Emmaline, was born on May 21, 1990. The father's identity remains undisclosed.
(From the collection of Marianne Williamson)

Marianne with her daughter, and friend David Kessler, at India Emmaline's first birthday party, at Orso's Restaurant in 1991. Kessler is the child's godfather.
(From the collection of David Kessler)

Marianne with Emma and mother, Sophie Ann.
(From the collection of Marianne Williamson)

With Sam Williamson, the "armchair revolutionary" who raised his kids in the political liberal tradition. Says Marianne, "I was raised to forge a revolution."
(From the collection of Marianne Williamson)

With David Kessler at a November 1991 dinner at the
Bonaventure Hotel honoring Elizabeth Taylor.
(From the collection of David Kessler)

Despite her glamorous appearance and powerful connections in Hollywood, Marianne Williamson insists that her personal appeal is not the point. She is no New Age guru, she insists, only a fellow student "giving a book report."
(From the collection of Marianne Williamson)

to offend my teacher, that was my problem. Marianne would much rather have people on an equal footing with her. . . .

There was a time when I felt the need to be very apologetic to her, and this was around me not being the person she needed in the work setting. I must have apologized to her two hundred times, so one night at the break during a lecture, she came down from the podium, took my arm, and walked the full length of the church with me. It was a big, cavernous church in mid-Wilshire. I felt like this walk I was taking with her was one hundred miles, and she said, "Susan, you must stop apologizing. Because every time you do, it opens up an old wound for you and it's painful for me to hear it. And you haven't done anything wrong." I was reenacting my hurt feelings and guilt because I felt I hadn't done a good job for Marianne when I was her personal assistant. Years later, I was still apologizing, droning on. It was one of the most loving things anyone had ever done for me. It totally freed me from ever having to say I was sorry to Marianne ever again.

Phelan was also impressed by Marianne's "amazing level of integrity, particularly where money is concerned. That shows in terms of the donation at the door being nominal and no one is ever turned away for lack of funds. The word 'no' does not cross her lips when it comes to giving. If someone comes to her and asks for something, she either gives it or says, 'Let's do it.'"

Phelan recalls an occasion when ten or so people were assembled at Marianne's apartment for a Sunday prayer group. "A little black boy came to the door selling candy," she remembers. "No one wanted to buy it, and here we were having a group on *A Course in Miracles*. Marianne immediately went to her purse, got out her money, and bought the candy bar. Then she turned to all of us and said, 'Come on you guys, you must never say no to angels, and you never know how an angel is going to appear.'

"I carry that with me," Phelan says today. "That tone has held throughout her ministry. I've seen her do things like that time and time again. People who were ill, she would take into her home. People who had no place to live slept on her living room floor. I knew that if I ever needed anything from Marianne, I could go to her and I wouldn't be turned away."

Phelan worked for Marianne for about a year:

Then we decided mutually that our interests were better served if we didn't work together and were friends and colleagues, in the sense of working toward common goals. Because of my background and personality, I felt I had more to offer than picking up her laundry, and she agreed. It was a liberating moment for both of us, and she addressed it. It was really quite wonderful; it was another gift Marianne gave me, because I would have

stayed forever and stayed small. By being allowed to leave her in the spirit of friendship
and love, it allowed me to take my lessons
with me and really grow beyond that. I regret
leaving her, though, I really have to say. I
wish I would have had the wherewithal at
that time to be that kind of person who could
serve her. Whoever would be that close to
Marianne requires a very unique personality. It would be someone who could read her
mind and then go off and work independently, and, at the same time, allow her
complete control. It's hard, it's a very tough
balance. But with a greater degree maturity
on my part, knowing what I know about her,
and knowing what was required, I could do it
now.

"Susan Phelan is great," says Marianne. "She
wasn't great at the time, but she's great now. She's a
wonderful woman; I really love her a lot."

After Susan Phelan, Mimi O'Connor worked for
Marianne from 1986 to 1988. "By that time I was
already over at the church on Highland and Franklin," Marianne recalls. "I remember her saying to
me, 'I'll do anything for you. If you want me to come
over and just do your wash, I'll help you.' I said, 'I
can use you. Help me, help me.' "

O'Connor remembers being on the telephone constantly. "People would watch Marianne's half-hour
cable access program and call the office. 'What is
this?' they'd say. 'What is the *Course in Miracles?*

Who is she? Where can I hear this?' It was amazing. So I had the gargantuan task of trying to explain in three minutes or less what the *Course in Miracles* was. It was very dependent in my mind on who was calling. Because they would preface it with such things as, 'Well, I was raised as a Jew and I've rebelled,' or 'I was raised as a Catholic and I've rebelled.' Myself being a rebellious Catholic, I was better at that one. Of course, people called because they'd been to the lectures and just didn't know who to talk to when they had a problem in their life. Somehow they would think of Marianne and they would call her number. I'm who they got, poor people."

The job also involved a good deal of phone counseling, "because Marianne would just reach into people's hearts in those lectures. I guess they always thought that she would listen."

Marianne's office was still in the second bedroom of her small apartment on Hayworth. During O'Connor's tenure, Marianne moved to a larger two bedroom condominium on Selma (which she left in July 1992, to move into her first house). The second bedroom, which became her daughter's, was the office. O'Connor says:

> I felt like a watchdog for her. She was an endless resource for people. If someone needed something, there was nothing in Marianne that could say, "Well, call somebody else." She would say, "I'll make time. Let's squeeze you in this half hour be-

tween . . ." It was insane, and I would yell
at her. I didn't want her to get burned out.
She's from really good stock, aside from her
amazing spiritual potential, and, of course,
one shores the other up. But she was end-
less and counseled people at the weirdest
times, at the weirdest places, and at her lectures, before her lectures, after her lectures,
during the breaks. It never ended, and I
guess I took up a little bit of the slack during
the day by virtue of her being out running
around so much, administering to whatever
it was. She was creating an energy that people were responding to, and there was so
much need out there. People would call the
office and I would get a chance to chat with
them, but invariably she would call them
back, just in case there was something they
needed. Or she would be on her way out the
door and I'd be saying, "You have to go, you
have to go," but she'd get on the phone. She
was so available to people. She was a never-
ending well. I was there night and day and
was witness to how much there was. People
going through every possible thing you could
think of, just trying to make sense of their
lives: money problems, relationship problems, AIDS.

Like Phelan, O'Connor was struck by Marianne's
generosity:

She always paid me well. She wanted to give me a raise too often. I'd say, "Marianne, it's enough." She'd say, "Come on Mimi. Loosen up." And I'd say to myself, "Omigod, I'm arguing with you not to pay me more."

She always answered to where the need was, and, remember, this was before her book. She made some money from her lectures, but there was never anything left. We'd always come down to the penny, because if someone said, "My mother's dying, I haven't seen her in a year, I don't have any way to go," Marianne would say, "Here." I would be crying, "I have to pay this bill and that bill!" "Mimi, lighten up," she'd say. "It'll be there," and it always was. I can't remember a time when it wouldn't come in or somebody would write a letter saying, "You spent time with me two months ago and I was so broke, I couldn't give you anything," and they'd enclose a check. She'd say, "I told you so, Mimi," and then call to thank them. It really was amazing; not like anything I've seen anywhere else. She always had free-will offerings at her lectures. There was a suggested donation, but many people didn't give anything and some people gave more. But it always worked out and she was always writing checks for other people. It was a nightmare trying to balance her accounts. Now it's much better for her because of her book. There's no doubt in my mind [that she's giving a lot of it away]. She had the faith and always knew it would be fine. And it was. Running her office was a little nerve-racking, but she taught me a lot, she really did.

O'Connor was an actress at the time, "struggling with myself and trying to find that degree of self-esteem to be able to do what I wanted to do. Marianne had less fear than most women I know. She was totally Marianne. I found that totally refreshing, because I was more of a person who wanted to please people. So here I see this woman who just answers from her truth. I'm not saying she's always right, but she just always answers from what she feels at the moment. There were many times when she took it back, said she was wrong, but she always answered from her truth. It was a spontaneous kind of courage and it had to come from a confidence, otherwise it would have been false. It wasn't know-it-all; it just came from what was true for her at the time. Sometimes her personality was strong, hard to take, and just cut through the bullshit. She has a temper, and people who were real close to her felt they should be exempt," O'Connor says with a laugh.

She would just have intolerance for something and let it loose. She's a very dynamic person and so it would be powerful. I had no problem with that at all, because I thought to myself, "This is great. She just lives constantly full-out." And I don't think I was living full-out at the time. I didn't know that, but I had to grow into my own skin. I've always been a very independent, assertive woman, but I had some extra things to learn about being assertive and independent from Marianne. Just when I thought I had it— other people would look at me and go "Wow!" I looked at her and thought, "Omigod, that's really fantastic."

She really is a personality. You could never say Marianne is a dull person, she's too alive, she's bursting at the seams and sometimes she'll burst all over you. At the same time, she was always encouraging you to grow past what you were. So she was really open to any input you could give. She wanted you to get better than the job. But there were certain things she wanted done a certain way, and she would have a fit if they didn't come out that way. And maybe sometimes she wouldn't even listen right away for the explanation. But she would always listen later. No matter how inappropriate I thought her response, never once did she not eventually come full circle, and usually within a very short time. She would just react very powerfully and it would be very off-putting, like you'd just been run over.

Like Phelan, O'Connor had to "grow up" to her employer if she would stay in the situation. "After a while I didn't know if I could work for Marianne and survive if I didn't learn to operate more fully out," says O'Connor, who is presently studying for a graduate degree in psychotherapy. "Because I think otherwise you may be swallowed up. So I had to reach down and come up."

> I remember initially I was tender and I'd get nervous. I grew up with a very angry father, and somehow this was hitting those buttons. I wouldn't say she was angry all the time, but she was sharp and to the point, it was like "get it or get off." We had to have a talk about that, and she copped to it immediately. "Mimi," she said, "I gotta tell you. You sort of protect your soft spots and come on, you're not as little as you think." And I thought, "That's really true." So I got a little tougher and she definitely got softer with me. Marianne and I just grew and grew.

Rich Cooper, a godfather to Marianne's daughter, had been studying the course on his own for several years, unaware that a community of like-minded souls existed in Los Angeles until he noticed an ad in a New Age publication for a Monday night prayer group (located in David Kessler's apartment). He says today:

> I wondered what she looked like. I pictured an older, heavyset woman with gray hair. Then Marianne walked in wearing this black knit long dress, very simple and casual. She

was like a light in the room. I had no idea
what to expect. I'm Jewish, and so the
course was always "iffy" for me. There was a
part of me that withheld from it because of
the Christianity. Toward the end of the evening I got up enough courage to tell her
about being Jewish and that I just couldn't
get past this. I didn't even know what hit me,
but she took so much time, at least half an
hour, talking about Judaism. She told me
she was Jewish and she understood. From
that moment I didn't feel nervous about
studying the course, and I was able to go
more deeply into it. Then I went to her lecture. It was surprising because I had felt so
alone in studying it. It was one thing to
study it by myself and another to hear it spoken. I had a million things to ask. If someone
was being shitty to me, how could I forgive
that person? She was the only person I ever
met who was ahead of me in the material
and could say "I've done this and it worked
for me." I gained courage to try out what I
had been reluctant to do just from listening
to her . . .

A lot of people read that course for years
and still skip major steps. That's why I think
Marianne is so misunderstood. Because she
talks about not skipping the steps in her lectures, and she doesn't want to skip the steps
in her life. I think a lot of people want her to
be an enlightened master. A lot of people say

she doesn't practice what she preaches because she gets angry. But if you understand *A Course in Miracles*, it's so much more than that.

As her audience grew, people asked to have tapes of her lectures. Steve Sager, who helped Marianne set up her tape business (they sell for seven dollars each) says, "So many people have been affected by those tapes, it's the thing in the morning that gets them going." The audiocassettes, which bookstores across the country just recently began selling, were hot items early on in Los Angeles. Popping a Marianne tape into the car stereo on the way to work became a ritual for many.

In 1986 Marianne began packing them in on both coasts, when she began holding monthly lectures in New York.

Ellie Ellsworth, who helps organize Marianne's lectures in New York, met her in September of that year. "I was in the most stressful and painful time of my life, involving the death of someone and the breakup of a relationship at the same time," Ellsworth recalls. "I was just on my knees, not wanting to live." Three friends independently called Ellsworth to tell her about Marianne's lectures: Jeff Olmsted, Marianne's former boyfriend; his wife Julie; and Charlotte Patton. "Not one of them knew I had a copy of the course or that I would have any interest in it," Ellsworth says. "But it happened that as I was going through this pain, I had picked up a copy of *A Course in Miracles* and tried it. Suddenly, after Marianne's lecture, I could read it, though I'd never been able to read it before."

Pat Buckley, a New York–based psychologist, had studied the course for several years with Kenneth Wapnick. While she was visiting her son in San Francisco, someone gave her one of Marianne's tapes. When Marianne began to lecture in New York, Buckley went, and eventually the two women became friends. She says today:

> Everybody has their place in this plan, and it's just perfect. Ken is a purist, whereas Marianne has a more humanist approach. Ken will use examples, but he will not compromise the course in any way. Marianne has just enough ego so that we can see, "Oh yeah, I know how that feels, that kind of thing." Ken helped edit the course, and he understands the course perfectly. It doesn't get distorted with him; there's no compromises of the purity of the teachings of the course. That's great, but then, I listen to Marianne and she's wonderful too. They both have their very wonderful parts in this whole plan, which is certainly not about ego's plan but the Holy Spirit's plan. Marianne has the ability to reach many people on a level of very human terms they can relate to. She does it with a sense of humor and an everyday way of putting things, so that the course principles become very easy for people to understand and hear.

In 1991 Pat Buckley's twenty-five-year-old son died unexpectedly. Devastated, she called Kenneth Wapnick. "I told him some of the images I had of Billy, and he said, 'Pat'—and he's said this before to other people, I've heard him—'don't be *A Course in Miracles* student. Be a normal person. Do what normal people do. Scream, yell, cry.' 'I couldn't stop crying, even if you wanted me to,' I replied. He repeated, 'Don't be *A Course in Miracles* student. People do misinterpret that; we cannot deny we are in bodies even if we don't have to believe that is the total truth about us. . . . Call me back,' he said. 'I'll be there for you.'

"Then Marianne found out and she called me," Buckley recalls. "We'd shared experiences before because I'd been on the board [of the Center for Living]. She prayed with me and she met me afterward, and she was really there. She's the humanist part. Ken was very clear—I couldn't read the course then anyway, it's too intellectual. But Marianne was on a totally different level; she was walking the trenches with us. She applied the course to the situation, but she also acknowledged the ego event. She's fantastic, she really is, and she's very willing."

Marianne considers herself "an orthodox interpreter, but one who is interested in contemporary and practical issues," she told a reporter from "The Bodhi Tree Newsletter." "I don't think of myself as a liberal interpreter in terms of the principles of the course," she said. "Sometimes modern seekers try to change the wording in primary-source material to make it a little bit easier. I don't mean easier to *un-*

derstand—but to *practice*. So, in that sense, I'm a literal interpreter of the course.

"The course says that love is real and nothing else exists, and there's no getting around that in staying true to the course. I try to apply those principles to various issues in our lives such as work, relationships, and health. But in terms of applying the specific principles of *A Course in Miracles*, I think that I'm rather orthodox.

"The *Course in Miracles* says that we're all students and we're all teachers—I'm no more a teacher than anyone else. What makes me a teacher of God is not that I teach metaphysical principles. What makes me a teacher of God in *Course in Miracles* terms is that I'm trying to be a more loving person every day.

"In the *Tao Te Ching* Lao Tzu says that a leader is not someone who thinks of himself as a leader; he is someone who considers himself a follower. In the Eastern tradition, the guru never calls himself a guru. I think that it's very important for Americans to respect teachers, but in terms of how I hold myself—first and foremost, I'm a student. There's no point at which you say that I'm a teacher now. If you do, I think you'd better look again, it sounds slightly ego-filled to say, 'Oh, now I'm a teacher.'

"I said something last night in a lecture that felt right to me," she continued. "The good teacher is not necessarily the best scholar of the material, but the one who helps you access the passion behind it the most. If you take a Russian literature class, the great professor is the one that helps you access the power and the passion of Dostoevski. At the same time, he's not claiming to be Dostoevski.

"I find it easy to get people excited about the course," she acknowledges. "I think of myself as a facilitator or a kind of midwife. When a baby is born, it travels down the birth canal to the end, and the midwife or doctor is ready to catch it. That's my job. I don't have anything to do with this birth of awareness, but hopefully, when you get real close to the opening, I can help pull it out.

"I also see myself as a sort of aerobics instructor. The aerobics instructor goes through the moves with you, and that's one of the ways he or she stays in shape, but she can't do the moves for you. Nor do I claim to.

"I'm just a student and teacher of the course," Marianne concluded. "I'm not a spokesperson for an organization. My mission is simply to be as happy and complete a person as possible. The more deeply I can achieve this goal, the more positive effect I'll have in this world."

CHAPTER SEVEN

SHEPHERD TO THE FLOCK

Marianne's audience spanned a variety of subsets within modern American culture—those fond of group therapy and twelve-step programs, those exploring New Age trends and offbeat spiritual paths, those disillusioned with the judgmentalism of conventional religions, and the lonely.

"There was a wonderful confluence of what Marianne had to say and what this community needed to hear," says film producer Lynda Obst.

Linda Ford, who has assisted Marianne on various charitable projects, recalls a lesbian wedding service at which Marianne officiated.

"This is what is so fun about her," says Ford. "She has so much space for people to be who they are. She's performed a lot of weddings, and she has no blinders when it comes to ethnicity or sexual preference. It was a beautiful wedding with two beautiful brides in long white wedding gowns with music and flowers. It was just like any wedding except there were two women marching down the aisle with their bouquets. Marianne made it such a sacred moment. She had so much respect for them and really was there for them. She made it seem like the most normal thing in the world. She did acknowledge that this was a little bit different and that she did not have the power of the state to call this a legal union, but she got people laughing. At the same time, she orchestrated it in such a way that it just worked. Everyone was really happy and it was a beautiful event. It was typical of who she is. She understands that two people love each other and want to make a commitment to each other and it doesn't matter what sexes they are."

"I think people are hungry for her message, very, very hungry for it," says Bruce Bierman, an architect who helped her start the New York Center for Living. "I think we all see that the world is dysfunctional. Then someone like Marianne comes along with a fine grasp on this set of books that makes sense to a lot of people."

A Course in Miracles refers to Jesus as our elder brother. Even though we're the same age, I always look at Marianne as my elder sister. One of the things I love about her is that she owns up to her stuff all the time. If she's wrong, she's the first to admit it, which I think is a rare quality. And she goes through things at lightning speed. I like being around that; it's inspirational for me because I see the attainments in her life as accessible in my own. It's about coming from love, it's about doing service, and you don't have to be perfect. What you realize is one of the reasons we're here on this planet is to learn these things. If we were perfect, I think there would be no need for us to be here.

She'll say something in her lecture and it seems so simple and yet it makes so much sense. I remember her lecture on the Gulf War, it was very profound. She talked about the amount of money being spent on that war on a daily basis. She kept repeating over and over, "Can you imagine what we could do with that money for the poor and the homeless and the hungry?" She talked about the good use of that money in a way that I could imagine what this world could be like. When she speaks, I can visualize myself being a part of it. It's not something abstract; it's something that becomes very doable in my life.

The most beautiful thing Marianne taught me is that the three most important words in the English language for me are "God, help me." The course says that a miracle is a shift in our perception. So, we simply have to be *willing* to be different. And she has such command of the English language, that to have someone like Marianne join with you in prayer is a very powerful experience.

Through her lectures and counseling sessions, Marianne was assuming more and more of a nurturing role with her gay audience, whose community was being decimated by the AIDS plague. At the same time, her close friend and personal assistant, Michelle Farmer, was battling breast cancer. When Michelle told Marianne that many people had helped her live, but now she needed someone to help her die, Marianne realized that type of help didn't exist.

One night in 1987, after her prayer group, David Kessler returned to his apartment and Marianne told him about Michelle. "A friend of mine told me, 'I have breast cancer and I really want to beat this disease,'" she said. "I had told her, 'Oh, there's all kinds of places you can go. There's Louise Hays [who had healed herself of cancer and held hayride/support groups for people with AIDS], there's the Wellness Clinic, this, that.' My friend has come back to me six months later and said, 'The doctors told me it doesn't look good. Now I need a place to help me die.' I realized there isn't a place, and I really want to start one," Marianne said. "Would you do it with me? Let's see what we can do."

"That sounds like a wonderful idea," he replied.

Kessler recalls that with himself as treasurer and Marianne as president, "We gathered together people who we thought would be good to have on the board, found a house, and had a fund-raiser at a private home in Hancock Park. That was how we raised the seed money for the Center for Living in Los Angeles.

"We wanted to get the message out that there is no situation that is hopeless, even when facing a life-threatening illness. At the same time, there is no failure in dying. We wanted a home where you could say the D word. People could talk about death, and by talking about it, our fears would be alleviated. We would grow more comfortable. We also wanted the center to be a space where people could do a wide array of groups. I remember going into that home and you would hear a mother talking to the mothers' group. She was now the volunteer leader, helping other mothers cope with their sons' dying because she had already been through that. It was just beautiful to work there."

Mimi O'Connor says:

> The need was so great, and there was so much coming Marianne's way in terms of "Well this is great and that is great, but how do I make sense of this horrible disease?" She was already running course study groups in which the people were HIV positive. She just went where the need was. Even her lectures always reflected what was happening in the news, because it applied to all of us and, the course principles apply to everything. There aren't any exceptions."

> I remember one morning she said, "I've got a really great idea. I said to myself, "Uh-oh," because that usually meant I had to do all the phone calling for her. "We're going to open a center; it's going to be great," Mari-

anne said. She was almost levitating she was so excited about this idea. She was talking about the Center for Living. "It's going to be great. We're going to get people like Louise Hays to be on the board and it's going to be a nonbedded kind of hospice thing. People are going to come there and feel better and get services for free." She was just rattling it off; I couldn't even listen as fast as she was saying it. My thinking was limited, but by modeling Marianne, I came to learn unlimited thinking. I was saying, "Oh Marianne, that sounds really great, but . . ." I was being the voice of what I thought was reality when, in fact, I realize now it was just fear and limitations. She'd say, "Oh Mimi, it'll work out." I thought there were huge obstacles like money, and she was just, "No, no, no, that's unimportant, that part's easy." So I said, "Okay, I'm working for you, go ahead, lead the way, show me." She did. That day she started calling people, they were immediately interested, and what happened since is history.

One of the first people Marianne contacted was Sandy Scott, the cominister of the United Spirit Church of Religious Science in Los Angeles, who had been doing intense work with the deaf and dying for several years since she had come to town with the controversial ministry of Terry Cole Whittaker. "She called Louise Hays, myself, David Kessler, a psychiatrist friend from Houston, and someone else," Scott recalls. "She didn't even name the center what she wanted to name it; she gave that power to the board. She was not on a power trip at all. In fact, she was very humble and sweet. She just says things the way they are; she's very direct."

"I remember when she got the idea for the Center for Living and announced it at her lecture," says Rich Cooper, Marianne's best friend. "It was to address grief and people with life-challenging illnesses. It would be not only for people who are sick, but people who are well, because we all minister to each other. No matter where you are on the spectrum, there's something to get from it. She created this context in which everyone could heal either by volunteering or by being a client. It didn't really matter. She presented it to the people at the lectures, they got excited, and a lot of life happened around it. Everyone who went to her lectures got behind it. I led a grief support group and HIV support group with Marianne at the center for years."

In fact Cooper's experience at the center led him to switch his career from advertising to psychotherapy, and he was able to spend part of his internship at the center, where he still volunteers.

"I volunteered the very first day the Center for Living started," remembers Carrie Williams. "It was this little house on Sierra Bonita: a table, one guy and me. That was the Center for Living; then it turned into an incredible thing. I volunteered every day, and I was in charge of doing the open house when it finally opened. The most amazing thing to me was that Marianne thanked me all the time. It was such a pleasure to do it that I was shocked at how grateful she was. She kept thanking me as if I was doing the most wonderful thing. She was very grateful for everything. When I first starting doing comedy, she would go out of her way and meet me at a club to see me."

Stuart Altschuler became the first director of the Center for Living in Los Angeles. He had been directing the AIDS unit of West Covina Hospital when he attended a Saturday morning lecture where Marianne announced that résumés in application for the executive director's position for the center were still being accepted. "I was there alone, but when she made the announcement, I heard someone say to me, 'Apply,'" recalls Altschuler. No one was sitting behind him, and Altschuler engaged in a silent argument with himself over whether or not he should apply. The voice came up again. "I said to myself, 'You're finally out of debt, how could you do this?' And the voice came again a third time, even louder, saying, 'Apply.'

"When I was hired by the board, I said, 'Omigod, what an incredible opportunity for me. I'm gonna be working with Marianne Williamson, Louise Hays, Sandy Scott. It's going to be peace and joy all the time," Altschuler says, laughing. "That was certainly not the case, and yet I wouldn't trade that year at the Center for Living for anything. It was a training ground and it opened doors for me."

When Altschuler assumed the directorship, pools of volunteers were already established, the house on

Sierra Bonita in West Hollywood had been leased and was being prepared, and Marianne was leading her weekly support group for those diagnosed with AIDS and other life-threatening illnesses.

It was already in motion, and I could have been carried away or run from it. I was very welcomed by all and it felt very good. It was Marianne's baby, and as with anybody who had invested and committed as much of themselves, it was hard to let it go. But she let me take it. I was a little hesitant. After I'd been there about one month, she sat me down and said that the center needed a strong head, someone people could really identify it with. She didn't feel I was doing that. She said, "You're either the person who can do it or you're not. If you're not, then we need to find someone else. You need to take charge here; this is your home. People are coming in and this is what needs to be done."

It was a wake-up call that I needed in a lot of ways. I made a transition and people started identifying the center not just with Marianne, but with Stuart Altschuler; and it really helped me put myself out there. I'm very grateful because it brought to my consciousness that I had choices to make. She even wrote me a note—I still have it—saying how glad she was for me to be there and that she'd like me to understand sometimes that this is her baby and just like any mother, it's difficult to put that baby in the care of someone that they're just getting to know. I really understood a lot about Marianne from that little note . . .

The center had a gorgeous backyard and a swimming pool and a great living room that you walked into and felt immediately at home. There were rooms for massage and rooms for counseling. It was a small house but we made use of every little piece of space. There was always somebody in the kitchen preparing lunch or Saturday night dinner, when we had professional entertainment. We sometimes had sixty, seventy people in the house on a Saturday night. It was like a house party every week.

Every week I was there hosting another get-together, one after another. We opened just before Thanksgiving, so we had a Thanksgiving holiday, a Christmas holiday, then a New Year's party, and it was really generating a sense of home: Come play with us, not just come and do your group work. It really is about celebrating life and celebrating celebrations and knowing that death is something that can be celebrated too. It was okay to use the word "death," everybody usually says they're making their transition. Sometimes you just need to tell the truth about it and get into your feelings in order to get past it.

People are still talking about that house. They're still saying, "Oh God, that house was so wonderful."

The center had rented the house on Sierra Bonita from Bob Gurston, who was at first very hesitant, but he soon became a volunteer, helping in the kitchen every Saturday night. When the center was told by the city they had to leave the neighborhood because it wasn't zoned properly, Gurston restored the house and moved back in. "He just died in the house about a month ago," Altschuler says. "It was sad, but he died with all that energy around him. That's what that house was about: massage, Reiki, rebirthing, counseling, chiropractic, and peer counseling. All that was going on, and it was a place where people could drop in, hang out, meditate in the backyard, and listen to music.

"All of this was Marianne taking her vision, making it manifest and surrendering to the form as it was changing," Altschuler points out. "I believe she originally thought it was going to be a hospice, then it turned into this, which was more incredible than anybody had ever dreamed. I had the privilege of actually being paid to show up there every day. There were times when I felt guilty for taking money because it was feeding me in ways that I never dreamed possible."

Tom Koontz, who is the current executive director of the New York Center for Living, had moved to California in 1987, the year Marianne started the Los Angeles center. When his friend became very ill with

AIDS, he sought consolation in Marianne's lectures. "Her lectures are extremely inspirational and take away the old myths that have been pounded into us," Koontz says. "I was brought up by a midwestern Methodist family. Of course, I didn't fit the mold for them whatsoever. Marianne gives a whole different take on what life, love, relationships, and people are about. It was refreshing to go to her lectures and hear about nonjudgment." As his friend got progressively sicker, Koontz began volunteering at the Los Angeles Center for Living.

I'm not really sure Marianne would want this story to be told, because it seems to single her out as having created a miracle, and she doesn't feel she's about that. But my friend had become bedridden for a couple of weeks and was suffering from systemic shingles. He was in a great deal of pain. I thought this might be the end.

I went to Marianne's lecture one particular night. After the questions and answers, I told the crowd that my friend was very sick and asked if they could include him in their closing prayer. They called him by name, and Marianne did a wonderful healing prayer with everyone joining hands. It was pretty intense. I went home and my friend was up making dinner for me. I considered that a personal miracle however it was caused. I've told Marianne that story before and she's very shy about hearing it. She has no ego connection to thinking she's a miracle worker.

Victoria Pearman had just been diagnosed with cervical cancer when she went to a lecture at a friend's urging and was immediately taken under the Williamson wing. "I was obviously very upset," Pearman recalls. Marianne asked what was wrong and then suggested Pearman call her the next day. "She focused totally on me immediately," says Pearman.

> She figured I needed help, and she was there for me though I was a total stranger. I did call her, and within a day or two I went to the L.A. Center for Living at the house in West Hollywood. She spent an hour or two talking with me about why I thought I got sick and what I wanted to do to change it. I think everything she said to me that day rang home. "I don't know," I answered when she asked me, "Why do you think you got sick?" I told Marianne I was in a relationship that didn't work and I had just produced a movie that I hated. I was really unhappy with the subject matter, which I thought was very dark and evil. I didn't want to make it, but the project was assigned to me, and being a professional, I took it on and did the best I could. "I have to make a decision in my life that I can't do that any more," I told Marianne. Pretty soon I got out of the relationship and didn't

have the operation I was scheduled to have, because I didn't need it.

I want to be very clear that Marianne did not encourage me not to have the operation. She was very supportive of whatever journey I would take, but she wanted me to be aware of the other side of it as well. I chose not to have the operation not because of her, but because I never believed the situation was as serious as I was told. But I was given the strength to make that decision by a belief system I didn't have prior to going to Marianne's lecture. She's not one who says, "Believe in this and you don't have to have surgery." In fact, four years later, she's the one who calls me every couple of months and asks, "Have you had your checkup?"

Valerie Lippincot, who later became Marianne's personal assistant, first heard of the course through the paper-thin walls of a rooming house when she was performing in a summer stock company. Someone was playing a Marianne Williamson lecture tape in the next room. "I remember I was sitting on my bed, feeling bad about something," says Lippincot. "I heard a woman talking about exactly what I was going through, and I ran into the room asking, 'What is this?' My friend said it was a tape on the *Course in Miracles.* I borrowed it and I really liked what she had to say."

When Lippincot moved to New York, she helped out at Marianne's lectures. "Sometimes we used to go out to eat afterward," Lippincot recalls. "I remember how funny she was, and we used to laugh a lot. She was tired and beat at midnight after giving this lecture and talking to a million people there, but she took time to listen to the volunteers. I remember thinking how wonderful that was. I did meet with her once, right when I first started volunteering. I had a lot of questions about the course, and she had me over to her friend's apartment, where she cleared them up. She was always very available, and still is. I'm still wowed by it even though I've been working closely with her for years."

In November 1988 Lippincot moved to Los Angeles and volunteered at the Los Angeles Center for Living. "I started working with people who had AIDS or were HIV positive, visiting men in the hospitals or in hospices. Marianne would sometimes have meetings for volunteers, and I learned a lot about listening, being compassionate, and not fearing death from her. That was one of the best times of my life. I didn't have a job yet, so I would spend my time doing work at the center. I was also making lunches or whatever. That was something she created and it was so wonderful, pure love. Everybody there was floating and getting so much help. That's something she created that I was really proud of."

In January 1989 Marianne's secretary at the time, Barbara Testa, asked Lippincot to work at the lectures. Then Michelle Farmer, who has since died, hired Lippincot to replace her as Marianne's personal assistant. Michelle had lived with Marianne when she was very sick. "It always seems that Marianne opens her home or her office when people are down on their luck," Lippincot says. "Lots of people have stayed at her home or office. I eventually moved in, running the office. So I've done every possible thing you could possibly do working with Marianne."

Lippincot recalls a time she made a serious mistake during a telephone conversation. "A boss could have gotten angry," she recalls, "but Marianne didn't. She let me know what was wrong, but she was into the solution and was really nice about it. She's always very fair even if she does get angry, or she lets you know what you did wasn't right and how to make it right.

"We have so much fun; we are the luckiest people," Lippincot says of her work today. "We work hard and there can be stress like at any other job, but there's so much support for who you are as a person. That's how it is in Marianne Williamson's office. That's why the center stuff"—the problems and negative publicity that would come later—"is so bizarre, because those people don't seem to know who she is."

In 1988, after one year of service, Marianne fired Altschuler from the directorship at the center. He was "traumatized. I would not have let go," Altschuler admits. "It was so nurturing and I was so hooked in. I can say in very self-centered terms what I was getting from being there, but with hindsight I realize I needed to be pushed because it was time for me to move on to other things. I would not be doing what I'm doing now if I had not left the center."

The center had expanded with lightning rapidity. It required a director with keener administrative skills. Altschuler's interests lay more in the human service aspect of the organization. "It became frustrating to myself, to Marianne and the board, and, at the same time, I think many people were able to acknowledge how much I was accomplishing," says Altschuler.

"I couldn't speak to what she's done with other people," Altschuler says, referring to publicized conflicts between Marianne and subsequent directors of the center. "I can only speak to what my experience with Marianne was. With each step of the way, it was a detoxing out of a lot of old stuff for me in terms of relationships and patterns. I was so conscious at this point, and had so much support from so many people, otherwise I could have taken a very different route. There were people who wanted me to do all sorts of crazy things . . . like go to the newspapers. First of all, I didn't see something on that level going on. I knew it wouldn't serve me, it wouldn't serve the center, it wouldn't serve Marianne, and, ultimately, it wouldn't serve the clients. But what I was going through was the same thing Marianne had written to me about when I first started working at the center. It was about letting that baby go to the hands of someone else. Then I really understood, because I felt at that point that I had raised this child and now, as I saw it at the time, someone was taking my child away from me. It was a grieving process that went on for a good year. On a very spiritual level, though, none of this is about Marianne. It's all about my own stuff, what I needed to do for my own growth, and I still learn from her. She's never stopped being my teacher, one of many."

After Altschuler left, Heath Hanner, who had a strong business management background, was hired, along with Jodie Schor as clinical director. The center had been given six months to move from the neighborhood. Hanner then got married (with Marianne officiating) and moved to Santa Barbara, so she resigned from the executive directorship.

When the center left the house on Sierra Bonita, the office and the groups moved temporarily into Marianne's office, a little apartment next door to her home. That helped the center continue until they found its present-day location, 650 North Robertson at Santa Monica Boulevard. While it lacked the Sierra Bonita site's homey feeling and its beautifully vegetated back garden with a pool, the Robertson location had adequate space for groups, massage, individual counseling, and administrative offices.

In the meantime, the Center for Living started Project Angel Food, a free home-delivery meal service. According to Kessler and Norma Ferrara, Marianne's "California mother," the idea was Michelle Farmer's, "who brought the idea because it was needed in L.A. In San Francisco they had Open Hands, and in New York they had God's Love, We Deliver." Kessler and Farmer flew to San Francisco to see Open Hands in operation, and then started the project in the kitchen of the church at Fairfax and Fountain, in West Hollywood.

Dick de Vogeleare, who became the third executive director of the Center for Living and who is now estranged from Marianne, recalls that the idea for Project Angel Food was his. Most likely the idea occurred to more than one person simultaneously; it was, after all, the next logical step in serving those suffering from AIDS. "Marianne managed to get it going," says de Vogeleare, "but the idea was mine, only because I had seen articles about similar projects in New York and San Francisco. I said to Marianne, 'We must do this thing,' and the moment I said it, she got right on the phone to the father over at St. Thomas Church and asked, 'Could we use your kitchen?' Then she called another lady and asked, 'Would you cook?' She's remarkable at getting things going. All she has to do is make an announcement at her lectures. I could get up there and say, 'We're going to start Project Angel Food,' and I wouldn't get any response. Marianne gets behind something and everyone's excited to do it. That's part of her charisma. In those areas she's wonderful."

Every day from early morning until dusk, the kitchen at St. Thomas bustles with preparations for the four hundred meals—lunch and dinner—presently being delivered daily to those who are too ill to leave their homes. Teams of volunteers prepare the food, pack the meals, and assemble bouquets from the flowers donated by local florists. "When they get flowers, they call up weeping," says Freddie Weber, the director of operations. In the auditorium outside the kitchen, brown bags are stacked on folding chairs, each labeled with their destination. They are picked up for delivery by another set of volunteers. Another team of volunteers cleans up. Every trace of the complex Angel Food operation must vanish by five-thirty or six P.M., in time for an Alcoholics Anonymous group to take over the space.

In 1988 Marianne approached David Kessler again. She wanted to start a Center for Living in Manhattan. The only problem was that there was no money for a payroll. "Well, you certainly need money for staff," Kessler said.

"Why don't you and I put in our money until it's up and running," Marianne suggested, "and pay for the staff ourselves?"

"That's what we did," Kessler recalls. "Those are the kind of things she's done and there's never any hoopla about it. She makes sure there isn't.

"The woman has a heart of gold," Kessler continues. "I remember one time, late at night in New York when it was freezing cold and we were walking down the street. There was a man curled up on the sidewalk. 'We've got to give him twenty dollars!' she said. 'Marianne, he's sleeping!' I said. 'He's not asking.' 'No, we've got to help him!' she insisted. 'All right,' I said, and I went over to give the man twenty dollars. He woke up scared, thinking someone was stealing from him. 'What are you doing?' he wanted to know. I said, 'We're giving you some money.' 'Oh, okay,' he said. I thought to myself, 'We're endangering our lives to help this man, and he's not even asking.'"

For several months Marianne and Kessler flew back and forth between Los Angeles and New York at their own expense to get the New York Center going. Marianne enlisted the help of her friends there to form a board of which she was president and on which Kessler served for a year until the center was fully functional.

Architect Bruce Bierman served on the New York board for a few years. "Marianne inspires people around her to come from their best," he says. "Marianne expects an enormous amount from herself, and because of that, she expects an awful lot in a good way from the people around her."

Marianne had called Bruce Bierman in May 1988. "I feel moved to start a center in New York," she announced. "Would you help me?" Bierman, Cynthia O'Neal, Michael Knapp, Paul Worner, Alan Pressman, and Pat Buckley met around Bierman's dining room table, and the center's first groups for those diagnosed with life-challenging illnesses were held in Bierman's loft. "Marianne would always remind us that we were just vessels," Bierman recalls, "that this was God's project, and it was important to keep our egos out of it. We would always start our meetings with a prayer."

Cynthia O'Neal, who later left the Center for Living and started Friends In Deed, her own AIDS charity, knew Bruce Bierman and was asked by Marianne to help raise seed money: O'Neal was already serving on the board of directors of the Healing Circle and was well-connected to the AIDS community in New York. She and her husband, actor and restaurateur Patrick O'Neal, arranged a dinner in fall 1989 at the Ginger Man and invited a group comprised mainly of theater people, including Mike Nichols, Carly Simon, and Judy Collins, whom O'Neal thought would be moved by the project enough to write a check. O'Neal served on the center's board and then became program director.

The group had raised approximately ten thousand dollars when they found a space, but they were unable to secure it without collateral. Marianne called her friend, Hollywood mogul David Geffen, from a telephone booth on Twenty-third Street. "David, we saw this building," she said. "Could you help us out? Would you be willing to cosign a loan with us?" Instead, Geffen offered a matching fund of fifty thousand dollars. If the center could raise fifty thousand dollars, Geffen would supply another fifty thousand.

"I remember when we were trying to raise money to match David Geffen's money," Bierman says. "We were somewhere between seven and ten thousand dollars short. Marianne made an announcement at her lecture, saying, 'We are short of our matching grant. We need help. If anyone can donate anything here in the room, we would really appreciate it.' A number of people made small donations and two people came up to us and said, 'Tell us what you need.' One of those people ended up writing a check for the entire amount.

"It was very clear to me that miracles do happen if you allow the space for them," says Bierman today. "That's the kind of thing that impresses me. Her visions are very focused. Just hold that vision and do it for the right reasons. I have never felt that Marianne is in this for herself. It's just what she feels she should be doing. I'm proud of her, and I'm proud to be around someone who does things like that."

Despite the obvious affluence of her audience and supporters, Williamson was clearly not out to make a profit. Many people did not pay the suggested donations at her lectures; some even received the lecture tapes for free. Her services were free, including the HIV-positive support groups and prayer groups, as well as her funeral and wedding services. Often, people didn't pay for individual counseling—and if their problem was financial, she would give them a check herself! Rather than take a salary from the Centers for Living, she put money in. She drove a battered black Peugeot, and her stylish image was created from designer clothes purchased at discount stores. "People at CASA"—a talent agency— "keep telling me 'She's a gold mine!'" said Steve Sager, who helped promote her tapes. "I think they mean she needs to be marketed—big. Tapes, direct mail, video, radio shows, television shows . . ."

But Marianne was uninterested in celebrity or self-promotion. She never encouraged her audiences to return or to bring their friends, and until she saw the need to promote the Centers for Living in order to ensure their financial survival, she routinely turned down overtures made to her by network television shows.

CHAPTER EIGHT

IMMACULATE CONCEPTION

On May 21, 1990, India Emmaline Williamson was born. Though Marianne has been linked with a number of men, she refuses to divulge the name of her daughter's father. Like so many of the women who attend her lectures, Marianne longs to be in a committed relationship; thus far there is no one. But she is devoted to her daughter, whom she calls Emma. Not long after Emma was born, Marianne had begun writing a book based on her course lectures. Despite the supposed glamor of her high-profile life, she was juggling an even more impossible schedule: lectures, charities, a book, weddings, funerals, counseling, and her daughter. She was still living in her modest West Hollywood apartment, driving the battered Peugeot, and stretching her budget to pay the bills. "She's a single mother struggling through—anyone who's walked in those shoes knows how tough that is," said her friend and course follower, Anthony Perkins.

"People are always saying to me, 'I keep attracting unavailable people,'" Marianne has said at her lectures. "I used to say that all the time. But you know what I found out? The unavailable person was me. The flip side of being attracted to unavailable people is how bored you are by available people. Available people are terrifying, because they want to hang around long enough to know you, to like you, to accept you. The problem is not that you attract unavailable people—the problem is that you give them your phone number." The line never fails to bring howls of laughter and bursts of applause. But as George Santayana said, "The same facts that make one laugh make one weep."

Marianne has been criticized for having too many boyfriends, for being a single mother, and for focusing too much in her lectures and in her books on romantic relationships, a subject that according to some is unworthy of a spiritual person.

But the course teaches that the temple of God is not found in our bodies but in our relationships. Our healing comes through our transformation of romantic or "special" relationships, which are enslaved to the fears of our ego, into "holy relationships," dedicated to God's will. Special relationships, according to the course, are those in which the ego deems another person as more desirable and therefore more lovable than others. Marianne's position on women and the current state of romance bucks the currently popular aggressive stance in which women defend their "rights" and refuse to settle for anything less than a perfect mate. "Do not

judge a person to see if they're worthy of your love,"
she says. "Love them and accept them first. I don't
think there are very many enlightened masters in
the major cities of America," she quips in one lecture tape. "It's not a matter of loving perfect people.
Love is the love of imperfect people, the point of
which is to love yourself. If you were to love everybody as they are, the ego says the world would be
chaos. The course says, excuse me, the world is in
chaos now. Without the ego, all would be love." She
says the course counsels that we release our relationships from captivity to the fear of our egos and
into God's hands. "Allow each other to be whoever
they are—that's the radical, nonjudgmental position
of Christ."

Though Marianne is unmarried and has had a series of relationships, the course says the numbers of
one's relationships or their duration are irrelevant if
love is present, and continues to be so even after the
form of the relationship has changed.

Norman Lear threw a party for Marianne in February of 1992 to celebrate the publication of *A Return to Love.* "Six boyfriends of hers were under the
same roof," marvels Al Lowman, Marianne's literary
agent. "They were, across the board, drop-dead gorgeous men. 'Marianne, how come they all came?' I
asked her, and she said, 'Because I always complete
my relationships.' 'That's a book,' I said. 'I think
that's extraordinary.' "

"The healings that came about in my relationships with men did not have anything to do with
anything I did differently," Marianne said at a

women's lecture intensive. "It had to do with my consciousness. As my consciousness shifted to forgiving men and knowing that they were as scared as we were, then my doingness took on a different energy entirely. When your mind shifts, your life shifts."

"I just ran into Jeff Olmsted, who was her boyfriend years ago," Ellie Ellsworth said recently. "They're very good friends, and, in fact, I introduced him to his present wife. Jeff's wife is a minister in *A Course in Miracles*–oriented church. They're very serious, spiritual folks, and he's very accomplished intellectually, very interested in men's issues and also made a tape using *A Course in Miracles*. It's a tight little network. As always, we say, 'Have you talked to her?' 'No.' 'Have you?' 'No.' She's a part of our lives, always. They had a very stormy relationship a long time ago, and they have become friends, more than friends, great, longtime pals."

Says another friend of Marianne's:

I've read some articles in magazines that state that her relationships do not work. Her relationships are extraordinary. Her relationships with her boyfriends are healed, they're in communication with each other, and there's a lot of love there. She hangs in there with people even if it looks like she doesn't. She knows her connection to these men. The course teaches not to get so hung up on form in a relationship. There is something much deeper going on. The only real purpose in our relationships is that we are there to see the innocence in each other, period. If it's in God's plan that we would get married or go deeply into it—great! But maybe we're only supposed to be brought together for a year or a month. That's not important. What's important is, will you hold to see the innocence and will you not cast that person out of your heart? You know the difference. You can leave somebody and cast them out, or you can leave somebody and say "I want to find the perspective and feel the love." I can say that has happened over and over in her life with different people.

"Rather than trying to keep it within a certain context, to force it to be something it isn't, Marianne always looks at relationships as an opportunity to get past her own stuff," says Minda Burr, another close friend. "It's not like there aren't any problems, there's always the opportunity to evolve, grow, and learn. There's always lessons there, and that's the way she looks at it." Burr continues:

She's a very emotional, passionate human person, and it's not like she doesn't go through painful experiences. She's very much dedicated to the *Course in Miracles;* she lectures the way she does because she is dedicated to living these principles. So she's constantly practicing what they're about, even when they're hard for her. She's always in process in relationships; she knows that's what it is. Like everyone, she'd like to meet someone and share her life with him. However, she's not looking for somebody to fit her picture, because she knows that's not taking the high road. She wants to love and be loved, like everybody else, and that's why she's able to change context. Her relationships are deep and they're powerful, and it's not like there's necessarily always an instant transition. It's important not to separate Marianne from other people, because she's in process like everybody else. Sometimes there's a little bit of time that goes by so that there's a clearer perspective. But there's always communication. In her lectures, she says the time for people to abandon each other is not when they're breaking up. That's when you need to be talking the most. That's when you really need to clear the air, understand, process, and evolve. When you're breaking up is the time to be the kindest to each other. The greatest cruelty is when people abandon each other when they're breaking up. I think that makes a lot of sense. People carry so much hurt and pain with them, usually because of the way they broke up. If you're honest with each other along the way, if you're really sharing what's going with you, if there's no deceit involved and if you're dedicated to supporting that person you care about and you've cared about in whatever process you're going through, if it's done with respect and kindness, that pain and deep hurt doesn't have to last as long. And then it leaves the space open for the friendship to be there. . . .

She's a strong woman. She's done a lot of work on being a woman. In the last few years she has had a different take. She has a softness and she's learned a lot about men. She's going to be speaking more about that now. I think she's found several men who wanted to marry her and she might have wanted to marry. I think that hasn't played out in her life because she had to write that book, she had so much to do in the world that putting that much form into one individual may not be what was up for her until recently.

"God has been good to me," Marianne said in a lecture. "I've always attracted men who, when you tell them to do it, they . . . forget it! So there's always been support for me to change, but as I've grown in those spaces, people noticed. Give all you want even if they're not 'the one.' They'll fall away, and one that fits the system will come in. It's not, 'Are they the right one?' Ask if *you're* the right one. It always comes back to us in the course."

Writers of books such as *Women Who Love Too Much* aren't talking about love, she points out. They're talking about something else, "but I suppose the ego loves sound bites. Love that is given to get something isn't love. So when people say 'I've loved too much,' what they really mean is they didn't get the return on an investment or demand."

Charlotte Patton, who assists Marianne in New York, says:

> She's never set herself up as being perfect. She'll be the first to admit "Sometimes I can be a bitch." She has said that publicly and you can hear it on her tapes: "There's times I've been a royal bitch in my relationships and I realize that's what didn't work . . . you can't be a bitch all day long and then come home to your lover and be sweet . . . you need to treat everyone like your lover." She said, "Life started working for me when I started treating my lovers like my friends and my friends more like lovers." It means you expect so much from a lover, that they should behave a certain way, call all the time, and you don't expect those things from your friends. With friends, your attitude is whenever they call is cool and there's a nice easygoing thing.
>
> At the same time, you should treat your friends the way that you like to be with your lover, very loving and considerate, and treating them in a special, loving way. That promotes your relationships all the way around.

Not surprisingly, Marianne enjoys playing the matchmaker, and like everything else she attempts, "she does a good job of it," says Linda Ford. "She's always fixing up her friends. She's very generous with everything in her life—her money, her knowledge, her ex-lovers."

Linda says that when she and her longtime boyfriend broke up, "I was a complete basket case." Marianne "would call me up every morning and see how I was and pray with me on the phone."

Then a few months later, Marianne called and said, "I know you and your boyfriend just broke up a couple months ago, but I have a girlfriend that I would like to fix him up with. How do you feel about that?"

Ford said okay, "but actually I didn't feel real great about it," she admits. "I was trying to be like Marianne. I wanted to make it clear that I was done with him, although I felt a little weird about it. I felt like why should I stop him? She loves to fix up her friends. She wants to make sure that everyone is happy. And when you're not happy, no one else will take better care of you. She put me back together more than once.

"In the relationships I've had," Ford continues, "the breakups were often my fault even if it looked like it was his fault. I'd call her up, whining and moaning, and she would read the riot act to me. I would end up apologizing to him. She would let me see that I was the one being the selfish bitch. She's all about communication. Nothing goes unsaid or undone in her relationships. She completes them. She has a really great tape called 'Love Never Ends.' She talks about how on the physical plane it may look like the love is no longer there because the two people have separated. The truth is the love never dies. People may appear to separate but they never do.

"It's as traumatic for her as anyone else to separate a relationship, if not more so," Ford notes. "She's going through something like that right now, but she knows if it's not right, if it's not serving both their best interests, then it's just a process. It doesn't make it any easier, though, and that's why she's so great."

"I think she's one of the strongest people I've ever met," says actress Melanie Chartoff, who studied the course with Marianne in the early days. "She also has her dreams, her desires, but she shared with me as I shared with her, some moments of confusion and weakness. It was around a man at that time, this thing we women go through about the unavailable man, which makes for very intense feelings in us, which I guess is the feeling of intense competition or winning."

Chartoff recalls taking Marianne to a Hollywood party several years ago and being impressed by Marianne's indifference to star power in a starstruck town. "We went to the party with a very well-known film director," she says. "To me, the film director was pretty heavy stuff—wow!—someone I should be impressed with, but Marianne didn't really give a shit. It didn't faze her at all; he was just a guy who was doing *A Course in Miracles* with her. She was interested in another man who was going to be at the party. She was kind of into the pleasure of her indulgence, her obsession—it was interesting."

Chartoff recalls watching a taping of Marianne's at a church in 1987 for Marianne's cable TV show:

> I was kind of shocked; she had spike heels on and was incredibly well put together. There's nothing wrong with that: you don't have to be an ascetic, robed guru to be spiritual or to give love to other people. It was just interesting because it was a very, shall we say, *Dynasty* look. She was involved with a lovely man at the time. But during the entire taping in which Marianne was giving a brilliant lecture on romance as laid out in the *Course in Miracles*, she was so angry at this guy that when they would break, he would come forward and she would chew him out so angrily. It stood out in bas relief . . . to what she was talking about: love and forgiveness. Obviously she was not forgiving him for something. She's constantly deflecting, though, saying "I'm not the *Course in Miracles*." But it's such a brilliant way that it's almost more captivating than the course, because she's a living, breathing, brilliant interpretress, and gorgeous, just adorable, and a single mother, which is probably one of the more heroic acts.

Suzanne Hoffman was taping that 1986 lecture and recalls the incident. The boyfriend in question,

Dwier Brown—an actor who has appeared in several films, among them *Field of Dreams*—was helping to make Marianne's tapes at the time. Marianne was upset not because of any personal problems with Dwier, but "because somebody was supposed to cue her that we were ten minutes away from the end, and they hadn't cued her. She'd gone about thirty minutes, and she knew she had to wrap up the introduction so we could do the question and answer session. We were filming her live, in front of a full audience with a three-camera shoot. She was arguing about a technical situation, something that was going on that she needed to know so she could get it taken care of. She's a businesswoman; she knows what she wants and approaches it in a businesslike way. If she was a man doing what she's doing, people would say, "He's a fabulous businessperson." But because she's a woman doing it, she's called a bitch."

"She needs somebody strong and gentle," says Tama Walker, Marianne's childhood friend, "a lion and a lamb put together. She needs somebody who's really strong, and it's difficult to find men like that."

Marianne's need, though, is hardly unique. In fact, it's virtually emblematic of the post-second-feminist-wave generation, the "Amazons," as Marianne and others characterize them, who have internalized our society's reverence for the "male" traits of logic, success, and performance in the outer world along with a concommitant contempt for the "female" traits of nurturance, intuitiveness, and simply "being." For many contemporary women,

Marianne says, success in the marketplace has been purchased at the cost of their essential womanhood, the "gloriousness" of being different but equal, and the inspiration to soulhood for the man.

"When I really looked into myself, I found I myself was antifeminine in so many ways," Marianne told her audience at a Women's Intensive lecture in June 1992. "That's why it was so mind-boggling to me to realize I had this core belief about Mommy not being effective. I realized I would get respect and love for my masculine achievements. However, it's not the kind of love that keeps you warm at night. Being warm at night is no small deal. We need to be kept warm at night in some way, to keep the juice flowing. Our function on earth is to keep the men and children warm at night.

"A lot of times we feel we want to surrender in bed, but we don't want to surrender out of bed," she notes. "In bed, we'll say, 'I want the man on top, in charge, the dominant partner,' and I want a hint of 'He could be me if he has to be.' Out of bed, I want him to be the opposite. 'How dare he be stronger, meaner, dominant.' You're angry at a man out of bed if he is too macho, and in bed you're secretly angry if he's not.

"I remember saying to a man," she told her audience, " 'You're so much nicer in bed than outside bed.' And he said to me, 'You surrender to me in bed and not outside bed.' I was outraged. 'What do you mean, surrender?' But I had to admit he was right, that sex worked better than any other part of our relationship. What I learned was that surrender outside bed was not surrender to *him*," she clarified. "For the feminine force to surrender to the *masculine* does not mean for the woman to surrender to the *man*. Surrender to the feminine means surrendering to something inside ourselves. It is a decision to let someone else have their own strength, but when you are holding a place for someone else to have their own strength, you yourself are in the very same position to do that too. So the feminine role, which is the magnetic rather than the dynamic within us, is not an abdication of power. It's every bit as powerful, but it is an opening up of a different kind of power. It does have to do with saying that love is more important than anything else, and that we are more concerned with peace than with argument, with connection than with separation. We are here to remind the world of the heart connection."

"It does a disservice to her and to her message to separate her out as being so incredibly unique from the rest of us that she has different requirements," says Susan Phelan, Marianne's former personal assistant. "She doesn't. She wants exactly what the rest of us want, and that's to be loved unconditionally."

One wonders if now that Marianne is renowned as a spiritual leader, she may be more daunting to a prospective suitor.

Her friend Jaquel Prier says:

> I know Marianne is looking for a man. The same way I've been watching Marianne's career, she's been watching my relationship.

It's been a balance because I was going after a career for a while and she was going after a career, but we both wanted a relationship. I kind of let the career go aside so that I could develop a relationship. Now I've got the perfect relationship, and Marianne has the perfect career. She's worked very hard. She's put every effort she can to help other people and to do what she knows is right in her heart.

These wonderful men that she's had in her life see a very strong, positive, together woman who's up there doing what she needs to do. She's reaching everybody's heart. When they get involved in a relationship with her, they find out that she's genuine and very fragile. Because they see her strength, they don't see her womanhood and that she needs just what we all as women need. She needs someone to tell her she's wonderful. She can talk to a thousand people in a room and she can sit at a hundred bedsides, but she doesn't have that many people saying, "Marianne, you're so beautiful," and when she's crying, saying, "Marianne, it's okay." Men expect her to be this strong, powerful woman all the time.

I can see where Marianne gets torn down because men want the strength, but they don't want us to be more powerful than them. Marianne brings prayer into her relationships. Sometimes men don't want to sit down and pray. They just want you to get better.

Strong, powerful women who are doing as much as Marianne need more love and compassion on a personal level. She is an intense person, and she needs someone who is going to allow her to have that intensity but also bring out the woman.

"Marianne has been great to talk to about my men," says Ellie Ellsworth. "She's been a great girlfriend that way, very honest, with a very good psychic sense, as well as the course knowledge to offer me when I was blind about the men in my life."

At the time of the writing of this book, Marianne's relationship with a men named Ben was ending. When Ellsworth visited Marianne in Los Angeles just before the uprisings there in late April 1992, she met Ben. "I thought he had a lot of strength," Ellsworth said. "That was one of his assets. He had a lot of strength with her, but I don't know. I've seen her with several different guys over the years, and I've learned this from her: straight guys don't have to try as hard as women do. They can just sit around and wait for the women to come to them. They don't have to work at something. They say, 'Well, this is difficult, let me go somewhere else.' I think it takes someone of a rare breed to recognize who she is and say, 'I want to support that, I want that in the world. I'll give her what she needs.' That's a rare person, and there's probably only one or two of them around. She probably hasn't met him yet."

Marianne's relationship with Howard Rochestrie, an attorney who heads Mercer, the largest fee-only (noncommissioned) financial management consultant firm in the country, is a case in point. The two dated for eight or nine months before Rochestrie moved from Santa Barbara to Houston, Texas.

Rochestrie was visiting with friends one afternoon when Marianne's name came up during the conversation. Rochestrie knew about the course; he had read Jampolski's *Love Is Letting Go of Fear*, which is based on some of the course principles, and a friend had given him a set of the books approximately ten years earlier. "I'd like to give you this tape," a woman in the group said to Rochestrie, and as she looked at Marianne's picture on the cassette cover, she commented, "Now this is someone you should go out with."

That night Rochestrie had dinner in Aspen with two-time Tony-award-winning actress Judith Light, her husband Robert, and two of their good friends. As he walked out of the house where they were staying, Rochestrie saw a pamphlet on *A Course in Miracles.* "I said to myself, 'What a coincidence, I just sat this afternoon talking to some friends about the course.'" Over dinner, he told the group that an unusual thing had happened that afternoon. A friend had handed him a tape by Marianne Williamson. "My friends said, 'Marianne Williamson, are you kidding? We go to her lectures every Saturday!' Then Judith looked at me and said, 'You know, Marianne would be a good person for you to go out with.' 'That's what someone else told me!' I said.

"Then I told the story to another friend who is a psychiatrist in San Francisco, and he said, 'You're kidding! Marianne Williamson! I used to go to her lectures when I worked in L.A. She's someone you should go out with.' 'Allright,' I said, 'I give up.'

Judith Light arranged for Rochestrie and Marianne to meet on Labor Day 1990, over dinner with her and her husband Robert. Rochestrie was busy, so they didn't begin dating until January 1991. He recalls:

> We became really good friends and dated on and off for nearly a year. We just enjoyed a really wonderful friendship. She's quite an incredible lady. It was an opportunity for me. One of the things I found most interesting about Marianne is she really walks her talk in so many areas. She's who she is in relationship and with friends. She really applies the work she talks about, which was a very useful experience for me. I learned a lot about surrendering and trying to have another purpose besides just the boyfriend-girlfriend thing or friends. We always did what we thought was best in terms of how we could serve God, and it was a wonderful experience. I know there's been a lot of press about Marianne not having long-term relationships, but it was a great relationship for both of us . . .
>
> Neither of us held ourselves up as experts about relationships. I'm divorced. But we

looked at a real commitment to learn and grow together. Part of the gift of me finding a Marianne or her me was that we be the next lessons for each other to work out some of the barriers we always present so that we can allow love to enter. We brought the course in all the time. We were a normal couple, but every once in a while I would say, "Okay, professionally speaking, if you were coaching us, what would you say here?" It was funny, and she would actually wear a different hat, if you will.

But we were living in two different cities. So that was one of the major challenges of our relationship. Plus I was a single dad a good deal of the time. Whenever you're seeing someone on weekends or for a day here and there, there's a lot of expectations.

"But I learned a lot from Marianne about relationship," says Rochestrie, who became a course student while he and Marianne were dating, "how we get lost on the form and the picture of the way it's supposed to be. Everyone is saying, 'It has to be a certain way,' and then going through divorces and heartache.

"We're still in relationship," Rochestrie explains, "and the form of our relationship looks more like what you'd call friends right now. But it's a real caring for each other, and, of course, right now I'm busy and she's been on her book tour. So even if we wanted it to be more, it would be pretty difficult."

Was Rochestrie intimidated by Marianne's status as spiritual sage?

Even if she's up on a podium, she always presents herself as very human and another student of the course. Because of that positioning of herself, it was never "I teach it this way, so I know." She's a regular person off the stage, and obviously a quite brilliant and intelligent one. I think the distinction would be if she got up there and said, "I am the source. I feel *this.*" There's not a lot of *I*'s there with respect to the source of the information. She is always clear that the source of the information is the course.

Having someone who is prominent, famous, or recognized could be a threat to a man's ego. But it was an interesting lesson for me, because I also lecture internationally on financing, communication, and management. When I was dating Marianne, I learned so much about what it was like for women to be with me. Hopefully, the women I go out with now will benefit from what I learned from being with someone who is more famous than me . . .

She's a very caring person who expresses her feelings and cries when friends are hurt. A lot of our dates consisted of going with her to a funeral she was conducting. She's always giving. The only time we'd get together "for me" was the weekends. But she lectured

Saturday mornings and Sunday nights. Sunday afternoons she led an AIDS group, and usually there was a wedding or funeral or private counseling. We just included that as part of what we did. It's nice to have your relationship not just be about where we're going to go for dinner, what movie do you want to see? Teaching is a big part of my life, and it was a gift to be part of that process.

She gave a huge presentation on Easter 1991, but she doesn't get nervous. You'd think she'd be thinking about what she's going to say, but she'll get up in the morning and say, "I just need some time alone." She'll sit on her bed, put her head down in her hands, and just pray for two to five minutes. That's all she does to prepare.

Emma was nine months old when Rochestrie met Marianne. "She's wonderful, a really loved baby," says Rochestrie, "and Marianne encircles herself with some wonderful friends: Rich Cooper and David Kessler. David is like a father; he comes over even if Marianne's not there. We would be flying back from Texas and David would be there at the airport with the baby. She's such a cutie.

"The final chapter has not been written on our relationship," Rochestrie says hopefully. "She's a wonderful person and I still treasure our relationship. I don't want to speak of it as if it was over."

In 1988 four of Marianne's girlfriends had become pregnant. Marianne decided to hold a support group for them in her home so they could share issues and information and pray together. Minda Burr, who is now one of Emma's godparents, was the only one of the four who lost her baby. "I called Marianne first thing in the morning because I was cramping and spotting and I was in a lot of pain," Burr says. She was in her fourth month of pregnancy. "I'd called the doctor, who had said, 'Get here right away!'" Marianne dropped everything, picked her up, took her to the doctor, and held her hand through the entire ordeal.

Approximately a year later Marianne became pregnant herself.

"I really admired her," says Jaquel Prier, "because she would say 'I've got to get married, I want children, my biological clock is ticking.' Then she realized that she didn't have to get married to have a child. We were in Aspen together while she was doing the John Denver seminar when she found out."

The pregnancy was not planned, but Marianne was happy and quickly adapted to the situation.

"I didn't consider for a moment not having the baby," Marianne told *Vanity Fair*. "To me there's nothing sinful about having a child out of wedlock. For me, to have had a child and not be married is many things, but it's not hypocritical."

A few months earlier, in May 1989, Marianne's friend Carrie Williams also became pregnant, and she too was a single mom. "It was under really difficult circumstances," says Williams. "I ran to her lecture, talked to her outside, and she was with me every second of the way. She would have had me move in for the entire nine months. The last month of my pregnancy I did live with her, and it was really fun being roommates."

Carrie Williams recalls:

When we were expecting our babies, she was looking up everything in their astrological charts. "Okay, if the moon is here, and this is that." The night my son was born, she said, "I've got two people working on his chart."

I delivered January second. New Year's Eve she gave an incredible lecture. I had taken a separate car from her. I got to her house, and when she got home, I said, "Marianne, we're going to have the baby tomorrow." I went to bed for a while, woke up at five in the morning, and called my doctor. She and another friend took me to the hospital. She didn't even eat; she stood there, holding my hand from noon until I had the baby at two in the morning. Her boyfriend was there with us. I didn't let him in with me, but he waited for us.

She was in the delivery room when I had my baby. I couldn't have had anyone better in the delivery room. Maybe the father, but maybe not. I had a C-section. I don't know if I could have seen that, but she stood there, five months pregnant herself, and that experience was ahead of her. It was intense. In her words, "You were out of your mind with pain." Then she had me come back to her home with the baby.

"At the same time I was going through my pregnancy, a really good friend of ours was dying of cancer, and she also lived at Marianne's. This is the stuff that nobody writes about. She does it out of the kindness of her heart and out of love for her friends. That was a pretty heavy deal, but Marianne was there for me in every aspect. She fed me, and she did everything. When we both had our babies, it was incredible. My son is five months older than her daughter.

"She gave me a job when the baby was two months old. She wanted me to work for her. She's just an excellent friend."

I've seen her give money to strangers . . . everything in her pocket. We were delayed in the San Francisco airport because of the L.A. riots. So we got off the plane and Marianne said, "Okay, let's just have fun." She saw an ethnic store and wanted to buy me everything. I was really uncomfortable because she wanted to buy two of everything. "Don't you love this? Don't you want it?" The saleswoman had seen her on *Oprah Winfrey* and loved her, so as we were leaving to get the plane, Marianne saw her book next door. She bought the book, signed it, and gave it to the woman in the store. We got back on the plane two hours later with four more bags.

While Marianne was pregnant, she took time to lead support/lecture groups for the homeless mothers being helped by Patricia Shelhammer's Family Assistance Program. "The automatic assumption was that she had a husband. She told them no, she didn't, but she was going to take care of her baby," Shelhammer recalls. "They were surprised; they thought only poor people had to get by with that. I was proud of her for having the baby because she wanted it. It would have been easy not to, considering what she does, but she continued to lecture and travel, pregnant or not. She was very honest about it. I thought it was admirable because she certainly could afford to support the child. So, why not have the child before she can no longer have children? I heard in her lectures that her mother and father weren't all that pleased. There were many people I assume who would rather she didn't have the child."

Marianne was initially concerned about losing her lecture audience, and was relieved to discover that they readily accepted her eminent single mom status. *People* magazine was going to do an article on her at one point, says Jaquel Prier, "but when they found out that she was a single mother, they chose not to run it. They were thinking here's this world leader, and she's out there promoting sex without marriage. It's stupid. What came out of it was 'Hey, we can have our cake and eat it too. It's okay to bring children into the world. You don't have to be in a relationship with another person.' " (*People* would later run a highly critical piece in February 1992, timed to the publication of Marianne's book.)

On May 20, 1990, twelve hours before Marianne was scheduled to enter the hospital to deliver her child by cesarean section, she was producing and hosting Angel Art, a fund-raiser for Project Angel Food. The event was attended by nine hundred people instead of the expected six hundred, and they were all packed into a steaming art gallery. The next morning, at nine A.M., accompanied by former boyfriend, actor Dwier Brown, Marianne checked herself into the hospital and delivered her daughter.

Even after Marianne had her baby, Michelle Farmer, her cancer-stricken friend, was still living in Marianne's apartment, and she continued to do so until the last week of her life.

"Everyone was telling me, 'Oh, your life is going to change completely [when you have your baby]," says Carrie Williams. "And it did. But not with Marianne. Nothing changed. She was in the hospital for a week, came out, and her life began again. Actually, it was more amazing, because she also wrote her book."

Marianne moved her office into her home after India Emmaline was born, but that was one of the few conventional concessions she made to motherhood. The perfect single girl's retreat, so beautifully decorated in warm desert hues—by a close friend who has since died—would soon have a living room whose centerpiece was a hot-pink, toddler-sized roadster and a playpen containing a mountain of toys.

Though Marianne's friend Gary Donzig is the executive producer for the television sitcom *Murphy Brown*, the inspiration for the lead character's pregnancy was not Marianne. However, the idea for the character's protracted struggle to find the right name for her child did originate with Marianne's own indecision. Shauna Hoffman says:

> For the longest time, Emma went by India Emma Rose. Marianne couldn't decide what she should name her. Marianne named her but didn't put it on the birth certificate. It was at least eight months during which she was trying to decide. Her grandmother was Rose. There was a name she wanted to use but it was her sister's name, and in the Jewish religion you don't name a child after somebody until they're dead. So she couldn't use her sister's name because she didn't want to insult her, although it was the name she really wanted to give. Most people call her Emma, even though she's legally India Emmaline. She was afraid that India might be too strong for a little child. She asked me, "Okay, Shauna, is she India or Emma?" I loved India, so I looked at her and said, "She's India." She was fast asleep. Then she woke up and I immediately cooed, "Ohhh, Emma!" Marianne looked at me like "Sure, Shauna, now you know what I'm going through!" "I quit," I said, "I have no idea what to call her. The baby is telling me

Emma, we are saying India." India is a nice, strong name, but a psychic had told her that India Emma had been Emma in a past life, and that's why she was so easy with Emma.

Emma may lack an acknowledged father, but there is no lack of love in the child's life. For starters she has several godparents: Bruce Bierman, David Kessler, Richard Cooper, Norma Ferrara, and Minda Burr.

"My daughter's going to be in a therapist's office thirty years from now saying, 'And then she left me to go to all these fucking meetings!' " Marianne has quipped to journalists. Though she may not be *haus frau* material, Marianne's a wonderful and devoted mother. The prospect of an adult India Emmaline weeping on a psychiatrist's couch is an unlikely one.

At a lecture stop in Houston in the midst of her book tour in the spring of 1992, Marianne half jokingly told her audience that she was torn between buying *My First Hannukah* or *My First Christmas* for her child's first birthday the year before. "I couldn't decide, so I bought them both," she said. "It's important for me to know my child is Jewish, but be open to bigger ideas along the way."

"Her daughter is independent and so is my son," says Carrie Williams, who says she talks to Marianne on the telephone at least five times a day. "They don't want help. It's 'no,' they want to do everything themselves. They're not clingy, because they've been around a lot of people. Sometimes she talks baby talk to her daughter. She thinks she's the most beautiful baby on earth and she tells her that all the time. She gives her independence and loves her. Marianne's a very compassionate, loving woman, so, of course, it comes out with her daughter. The baby is very happy."

"We can't really give to our children what we don't have ourselves," Marianne writes in her book. "In that sense, my greatest gift to my daughter is that I continue to work on myself."

Marianne is determined not to repeat the child-rearing mistakes of her parent's generation. "This society doesn't give anyone permission to experience their emotions," she told the audience gathered for her women's intensive lecture in June 1992. "Emma was upset one day because she knew I was leaving. My girlfriend said to her, 'We're not going to have any crying today, no crying today.' She had never heard anybody say that to her, and I don't want her to hear that. You learn when you have a baby how incredibly cool kids are. Ninety percent of the time when my daughter cries, she has a very good reason. I just have to shut up and listen. She's frustrated: she wants to communicate but she's a baby, so she can't. All she was asking for was that someone explain it to her, and then she wouldn't cry. Once it was explained to her, even though she doesn't fully understand English yet, she got it. I addressed her issues, and she stopped crying.

"See how it starts?" Marianne asked rhetorically. "Then she gets the idea that expression of her emotion is bad. But that's what's so enlightening about this kid; she cries when she feels like crying. Children are so current. Yet we were all taught when we were little boys and girls—no crying, when there's such a wisdom to that crying."

With the aid of weekday and weekend nannies, Marianne continued her seven-day-and-night work schedule.

When Carmen, the weekday nannie, became pregnant, she took time off to have the baby and then returned to work with her infant son, Alexander. "Marianne wants Emma to feel like there's someone else who has importance too, so she doesn't grow up thinking she's the only little girl in the world," says Lippincot. "Emma loves him, and he's getting the same kind of attention she gets. It's one big happy family, a real cool environment to work in."

"Marianne's phone starts ringing early in the morning and does not stop," says Bruce Bierman. "I don't know how she does it. Her baby is very important to her; and she's a great mother. This baby is just the best. I just light up with this baby; she's just so happy, and Marianne's commitment to that baby is wonderful to watch, because she is doing it alone."

"I'm crazy about her," echoes co-godfather David Kessler. "She's beautiful, the happiest child I've ever seen. She's incredibly playful. It's been wonderful to see Marianne become a mother. Motherhood has given her an even deeper view of life and its preciousness. If anything in life is a miracle, it's having a child.

"She makes sure to fit in quality time for the child.

Her schedule is so tough that it can't happen accidentally. She plans and makes sure the baby gets the attention."

"She's always around," says Katherine Harvey, who works with Marianne at home. "Emma comes in to play and everything is dropped. She gets on the bed, they play for a while, the baby gets bored and goes back into the living room or goes to the park. Everything revolves around the baby, and everything else takes second place. When the baby comes home, Marianne goes into the hall, picks her up, throws her around, plays with her, and it's baby time. I follow Marianne with my notebook: 'Can we talk about this while you're playing?' Emma fits in totally and beautifully and perfectly. It's going to be fascinating to see her in the future because she has so much love from her mother, from everybody. She's like a textbook example of all the things we say we're going to do with our kids when we have them, the things our mothers didn't do with us."

"Marianne got more than she expected," says Jaquel Prier. "Emma is phenomenal. The child is a gift to Marianne, and she is really going to be something. Since she's had Emma, she's still very people-oriented; she wants to keep helping people, but the child brought out a new understanding of what being a woman is. She's always wanted a relationship with a man. I think that's all of our intentions. But being a mother has brought her more focus with being a woman and what it takes to have a relationship with another person. All of a sudden you become more patient and vulnerable when you have children. It might be in preparation to sharing her life even more. She's got so much going on. She really wants and needs a man to support her through the good and bad times.

"She certainly doesn't need anyone," Prier qualifies. "Her personality hasn't changed. In a sense, everyone Marianne spoke to was her child. Her attitude was 'I will care for you. Let's pray.' Now she has Emma."

CHAPTER NINE

FACE OF AN ANGEL

It was February 1991, and Marianne had spread her wings. Wearing a strapless, black sequined gown, she led a prayer as Hollywood shoguns Mike Ovitz, Frank Mancuso, Peter Guber, Jon Peters, Jeffrey Katzenberg, Michael Eisner, Penny Marshall, Jim Brooks, Jackson Browne, Joni Mitchell, Barry Diller, and Sid Sheinberg held hands and bowed their heads. The occasion was a gala birthday dinner for entertainment mogul David Geffen thrown at super producer Sandy Gallin's house.

Marianne was now lecturing to packed churches three times a week and running a weekly AIDS support group in Los Angeles. Once a month she was flying to New York to run her AIDS support group there and lecture at Town Hall. Crowds totaling at least five thousand were hearing her speak each month.

Lynda Obst, Marianne's college roommate, remembers attending a lecture where some audience members became aware of her connection to Marianne. "The sea parted like for Imelda Marcos," Obst says, laughing. " 'This is her roommate! This is her roommate!' I thought, 'God, I thought I did well, but, in fact, my roommate Marianne is God!' She saw me sitting there, came up to me and said, 'I always knew,' meaning that eventually I would come to her. She was right."

The Los Angeles and Manhattan Centers for Living, and Project Angel Food, were providing a wide variety of nonmedical services to hundreds every week. The 1990 tax returns for the Los Angeles Center for Living show that the group raised some $981,524 from contributions and events. Of this sum, $141,921, or fourteen percent, went to fundraising, and $94,157, or less than ten percent, went to management expenses. The total center payroll—including compensation for some seventeen employees—was $174,365. On the tax form, the center reported that "Assistance is provided to those with terminal illnesses."

Hollywood celebrities and movers-and-shakers were particularly taken with Project Angel Food. Bette Midler made a public service announcement directed by John Schlesinger. Angel Art, the fundraiser for Project Angel Food that had been held at an art gallery on May 20, 1990, attracted such Hollywood luminaries as Dennis Hopper, Teresa Russell, Meg Ryan, Twiggy, Arnold Schwarzenegger, Angelica Houston, and Elizabeth Taylor.

Actresses Raquel Welch, Roseanna Arquette, and Cher attended her lectures. Lesley Ann Warren called Marianne a "pal." Comedian Louie Anderson, actresses Kim Basinger and Angelica Houston, movie executive Barry Diller, designer/socialite Diane von Furstenberg, actress and author Shirley MacLaine, and artist David Hockney were serving on the Los Angeles Center for Living's honorary board of advisors.

While all who helped were not interested in the teachings of *A Course in Miracles*, dozens of other celebrities lent support, helping Marianne raise over $1.5 million as of March 1992 for her work on behalf of people with life-threatening diseases.

Some supercelebs, like Barbra Streisand, were interested in her teachings but reluctant to appear in public. So they bought the lecture tapes, of which there were over fifty titles available, including "Forgiving Your Parents," "Death Does Not Exist," "Fear of Abandonment," "Romance: Releasing Our Stuff," and "Anger." "You don't have to give up your whole existence in order to lead a spiritual life," reasoned actress Teresa Russell. "You can be semi-enlightened. That's sort of the message she's talking about."

"She's charismatic," says Tom Koontz, executive director of the Manhattan Center for Living. "She's a people magnet. I sat next to Cher at a lecture in California, and I saw Tony Perkins. Stars are always scattered in the audience. They're attracted because they're dealing with the same issues we're dealing with. I don't see what the hullabaloo is; some of these people are very supportive of the center. Cher sent us a large donation not too long ago. Bette Midler signed our year-end appeal for us."

"Tony Perkins is probably one of the celebrities you'll most hear about going to meetings," says friend Bruce Bierman. "When I met Tony and his wife [Berry Berenson], I could see why she would want to be friends with them. They seemed to be really great people. If you see the kind of people Marianne responds to, those are people you would want to know, whether they're celebrities or not."

Though later press reports would label Marianne star-struck, in truth she was caught in a double bind. "The bottom line is you can't be in the public eye and do what she does and not be famous," notes psychologist and Los Angeles Center board member Ron Gelb. "The more fame and notoriety she got, the more donations the Center for Living received. It rose in three years from a grassroots organization in the little house on Sierra Bonita where we ran a few groups and served a few meals, to serving almost four hundred meals daily, seven days a week. It takes a lot of money to run that, and this year [1992] the [Los Angeles] Center is probably going to be raising close to two million dollars. This is the second biggest AIDS charity in Los Angeles. A lot of what did come about was because of her notoriety."

Marianne had been lecturing in Hollywood since 1983. As she has said on numerous occasions, you can't do anything in Hollywood without running into media stars, just as you can't do anything in Houston without running into someone from the oil industry. Being part of the population, celebrities naturally came, but Marianne never sought them out. In fact, a major concern, a friend says, was that the public understand many of the stars were helping because of their commitment to AIDS and not to her personally. This sort of press could easily have frightened the celebrities away and consequently damaged the charities.

"*A Course in Miracles* teaches that people are people," Marianne finally responded to talk show host Larry King's persistent questions concerning her celebrity connections. "It's really just an illusion that anybody's different. I look out at one thousand faces a week and maybe one face happens to be someone I recognize. It's gratifying," she acknowledged. "The creative life is a vanguard position, by definition, so it doesn't surprise me that creative people are open to the cutting edge in thought and perspective. But we are all given that gift. We're all creative. What you and I call creative people are those who have accessed a creative flow that is in all of us.

"People are people wherever you go," she said in answer to another questioner. "They are all dealing with the same *mishugoss* [Yiddish for craziness] whether they're rich or poor. We're all hopeful and we're all tortured at times."

Tied in with the concern about her Hollywood connections was the undue attention paid to Marianne's stylish image. Bruce Bierman says:

> I love the fact that she's beautiful, dresses nicely, and that she has a desire to look her best. Why not? Doesn't God want us to be

happy, healthy, prosperous, and loving? When people use clothes as all-important, that's a problem. I don't get that from Marianne. Part of Marianne's appeal is that a lot of people can identify and respond to those values. I don't know what we have with celebrities or why we have to think shopping is selfish. Shopping does a lot of good. We can look at it as something that employs a lot of people, helps the economy, and helps us feel better about ourselves.

A few months ago when I started renovating my home, I became very depressed. I called Marianne and she helped me with this one too. I said, "Here I am spending a lot of money to put in big screen TV, a rug, furniture, kitchen, a new dressing room. There's a recession out there and I feel I shouldn't be doing this."

She said, "No, it's just the opposite; it's exactly what you should be doing. How many people did you employ this week?"

I said, "Well, there are six people in my office and then there were five workmen."

"Okay," she said. "You were responsible for eleven families paying their bills this week. If we all had a collective consciousness where we believed we were here to help one another, not to take from one another, then, when a recession hits, we would choose to spend more money to get the economy going rather than to hold back, which is what's happening now."

Marianne herself once held a similarly misguided puritanical view that abundance is somehow inherently sinful while poverty, by definition, is a purer state.

"When I was younger," she writes in her book, "I cherished the belief that, by being poor, I was somehow showing my camaraderie with the impoverished. Behind that thought, I see now, was my fear that I would fail if I tried to make money. I ultimately realized that poor people didn't need my sympathy so much as they needed cash. There's nothing pure or spiritual about poverty. We often see impoverished people who are very holy, but it isn't the poverty that creates the holiness. I've known some extremely spiritual wealthy people, and I've known some poor people who were anything but."

The media had anointed Marianne as Hollywood's latest guru, and that type of attention escalated after October 1992, when Elizabeth Taylor, about to marry for the eighth time, approached Marianne through their mutual friend Sandy Gallin to ask if she would officiate at her wedding to construction worker Larry Fortensky. "Her sense of spirituality triggered off my own," Taylor later explained.

"Marianne felt very honored to be doing something with Elizabeth Taylor because of all the work Elizabeth has done in the field of AIDS," says David Kessler. "After that, Marianne introduced me to Larry, who cleaned ovens with me at Project Angel

Food. He did it regularly, two and three times a week."

The Sunday-afternoon wedding—dubbed by Rod McKuen "The Taylor-Fortensky Wedding and Air Show" because of the platoon of news helicopters that buzzed overhead, took place on pop star Michael Jackson's 2700-acre fairy-tale ranch/estate, set in the Santa Ynez Mountains near Los Olivos, California, two hours north of Los Angeles. Marianne conducted the ceremony under an oak-shaded white gazebo covered with swags of green bearing giant gardenias and daisies and topped by a white pennant. Music was provided by a white grand piano and four violins. The wedding guests looked out on a view of beautiful trees surrounding a man-made lake on which floated a large, white swan boat, two green walkways of artificial turf that led to the gazebo, and the many brooks that intersect Jackson's property.

Wearing a beige Holly Harp dress, Marianne entered the gazebo, followed by Larry Fortensky in white dinner jacket, his best man—hairdresser José Eber—and Elizabeth Taylor in a tiered, buttercup-yellow lace, floor-length Valentino gown, escorted by her son Michael Wilding Jr. and Michael Jackson.

The remainder of the wedding party included Jackson, Brooke Shields, bridesmaid Carole Bayer Sager, and her man, producer Richard Cohen.

"When the helicopters were at their worst, after we got out there and the ceremony started, we saw that Marianne was concerned that people could not hear her, nor hear us," Liz Taylor told columnist Liz

Smith. "I said to her, 'Don't worry. We can hear you and that's what's important.'" At one point Marianne shouted out to the audience, "I know you can't hear us, but I promise you that Elizabeth and Larry can hear!"

After the ceremony, Marianne confided in her friend Linda Ford that "it was like standing on a runaway in the middle of a busy airport with ten 747s lined up behind you, trying to do a very serious religious ceremony."

"That's all she had to say about the whole thing." Ford says. "She was trying to make this a beautiful moment in their lives and the helicopters just wiped it out."

The Taylor-Fortensky nuptials were not Marianne's first celebrity wedding. Emma Walton, daughter of actress Julie Andrews and set designer Tony Walton, had been volunteering at the lectures for a few years when she was married by Marianne in what one onlooker described as "the most beautiful and personal wedding I'd ever been to. She didn't change the wedding because of who they were, but she did some wonderful things. She didn't just say 'Do you Emma take Steve?' She looked over at Steve's mother and said, 'Do you take Emma for your daughter-in-law?' and she looked at Emma's parents and said, 'Do you take Steve to be your son-in-law?' She involved both families so that there was even more of a sense of commitment and embracing of the whole family."

More impressive than Marianne's star connections, perhaps even more than her own charitable work, were the many who heard her message and were inspired to redirect their lives toward service.

Ellie Ellsworth put together a class called "Healing Singing," which meets twice a week for two hours at the Center for Living in New York:

> It's probably one of the most meaningful things in our lives, whether we're facilitators or those dealing with the various life-challenging illnesses. It's a very meaningful circle of prayer and singing, and everyone seems to get the notion of healing singing. By the time the two hours are over, people are joyful and laughing, have cried a bit and hugged, and have felt the power of prayer. In fact, I don't even know if Marianne knows this, but a documentary filmmaker is coming to make a film of it a week from tomorrow. Marianne created this incredible healing center. It's been part of her drama too, but I think that's because she hasn't trusted that it's really working and it's really all right. Now it's beginning to work at a whole other level.

Patricia Shelhammer was a church administrator who had rented space in 1983 to Marianne for her lectures. After Marianne gifted her with a copy of *A Course in Miracles*, she was inspired to found the Family Assistance Program, which to date has helped eight hundred families get off the welfare rolls and become self-sufficient. The only long-term support system in Los Angeles, the program finds housing and trains heads of household for careers. "The thrust is that these families should be empowered and change their image of themselves," says Shelhammer. "By the time they leave us, they are employed, off welfare, and supporting their families. We help the children get up to grade level in school and function again as productive citizens. We do tutoring, psychological counseling, parenting classes, self-esteem classes, whatever it takes."

Shelhammer says she was able to create and run the agency through Marianne's encouragement:

Most people were saying I couldn't or shouldn't, but she kept saying that she thought I could do it. She worked quite closely with me initially, helping and advising me. When I got stuck on problems on the course, she was always available. She was always very interested in making the course come alive for people, so she talked frequently in her lectures about the fact that people needed to be involved in service. Marianne and her group also put on many dinners for me. The whole group would cook dinners for my families on holidays. I asked her to come talk to my families on several occasions, and they still remember her . . .

There have been some tough times. It's all privately funded; there is no government money, especially in the past couple of years. My background in business taught

me that you always had to have a year's budget up front, otherwise I panicked and fell
apart. I've learned over the years and with
Marianne's encouragement to trust God and
it always comes from somewhere. She's also
been very generous financially, whenever
she can. We continue to operate and right
now I think we're in a pretty good position.

Shelhammer recalls in particular her first fund-
raising attempt in 1987. Lacking experience, she
was unable to sell enough tickets to the dinner at a
private home. Marianne brought a group to "paper
the house," including Linda Ford, who heads her
own public relations firm. Ford immediately volunteered her fund-raising services to the charity.
"Linda's Spare Change project, the fund-raising
arm of the Family Assistance Program, has continued to raise money for us ever since," says
Shelhammer.

A few years ago Shelhammer lacked funds to join
Housing Now, a march on Washington for the homeless, and Marianne paid her way.

Not all of Marianne's efforts to be of service had
positive outcomes. Reverend Sandy Scott, who
served on the board for the Los Angeles Center for
Living, was also president of a group of rabbis,
priests, and ministers who served people with AIDS.
When Marianne learned that the organization was
struggling to stay financially afloat, she offered to
help by taking them under the wing of the Center for
Living.

"These arrogant assholes said 'no' to Marianne,"
Scott recalls with anger. "She was going to embrace
this struggling, dying group and personally guaran-
tee them a seventy-thousand-dollar-a-year budget.
We had been out of money, so a rabbi had suggested
asking the Center for Living to take them on," Scott
explains. "The two boards met [at a room in the Roosevelt Hotel paid for by Marianne], and I was so
ashamed of my group that I apologized to Marianne.
The group didn't say yes because they were jealous
and scared. *A Course in Miracles* is New Age, not an
established religion. One man said, 'You know, I
don't trust you Marianne. Why are you doing this?'
She leaned over and said, 'Because this is the work
God would have us do, because you've lost all your
money and you need a place to be, and I'm willing to
commit seventy thousand dollars to you people to
come in. I will not control you. I will not try to ma-
nipulate you. I will give you a home, a budget, and a
staff person because I believe in the religions bringing people together and responding to AIDS.'"

Scott's group finally "lost everything," she reports,
"and now we meet every three months at a church
somewhere. The group doesn't have a home anymore."

Despite disappointments such as the above, Marianne would carry her work to another level. She
would touch millions with the message of *A Course
in Miracles* and inspire them with her example.

On a subzero, windy Manhattan night in January
1988, a literary agent named Al Lowman attended a
Marianne Williamson lecture. Lowman says:

Some wonderful person, whoever they are —and maybe they'll identify themself when they read this book—had put my name on Marianne Williamson's lecture audience list. One of those cards that are still issued by her office monthly for the New York and Los Angeles lectures appeared on my desk in December 1987. I was in a terrible personal crisis in my life at that time and looking for help—mostly in the wrong places. When her card hit my desk at that point, I couldn't resist the juxtaposition of a beautiful woman's face, the word "miracle," and the fact that she was in Rutger's Presbyterian Church in New York City, a small church on West Seventy-third.

I hauled myself over to Rutger's and shivered along with two hundred other people in that church. I'll never forget that moment, because I thought, "I can't believe I'm actually back in a church." I hadn't been in one since the age of sixteen, and by now I was almost forty years old. I looked around and saw the same faces I'd seen in every workshop I'd ever attended over the years. "Well," I thought, "same faces, more gray hairs, we're still obviously asking ourselves the same questions and not finding the answers."

Then this tiny birdlike figure came onto the altar and started her rap. My first reaction was, "Oh my God, she sounds so harsh." I guess she was strident-sounding, not what I thought someone in a Presbyterian church should sound like. I remember being disarmed by that, and being disarmed, I began to listen. The more I listened, the more I was actually blown away by her language, which seemed to be my language exactly. Everything she said, every word, every sentence, every thought, every concept, was what I thought I'd been saying to myself, or words that I wish somebody had used when I was growing up. I remember being so blown away that first night, and I don't remember what the lecture was at all.

Lowman kept attending the lectures and bought tapes. Then he finally approached Marianne to shake her hand. "Neither one of us will ever forget that moment," he recalls. At six feet, four inches, Lowman towered over the diminutive Marianne by at least a foot. "I looked into her eyes and she into mine, not as two potential lovers would look at each other, but with the look of destiny," Lowman explains. "It was that profound an exchange." As they talked, they discovered they had friends in common and that Marianne admired two of Lowman's clients, Carrie Fisher and Lynn Andrews.

A second card, this one announcing a Saturday Valentine's Day intensive for men and women, crossed Lowman's desk. It came "at one of the true low points in my life, that I would go to a workshop on Valentine's Day along with ninety-nine other wounded souls," Lowman says. "I thought, 'How perfect!' She did such a brilliant job during that weekend. The process is still clear as day in my mind. She separated the room into gender; men on one side and women on the other, and by the end of the day the room had been blended. Through a step-by-step process we found out what each gender had to say about the other, what fears existed, and why, perhaps, we were in that room to begin with. It was a very intense experience."

Lowman asked Marianne to lunch that day. "Marianne, I've listened to twenty-five, thirty of your tapes," he said. "I think you are an important person, someone who probably has a huge and impactful future in front of her. I think your book has already been written, and I'd like to represent it."

"Gee, that's funny," Marianne replied. "Two weeks ago Jerry Jampolski told me basically the same thing, that he thought it was time I wrote a book. Where do I start?" she asked.

"You start by trusting me," Lowman recalls saying.

The writing process turned out to be a good deal more complicated than their initial notion of simply transcribing Marianne's lecture tapes and hiring an editor to shape them into a book. "Marianne is like a jazz singer on stage," Lowman explains. "She zigzags and draws from many sources—not just *A Course in Miracles*—and makes so many references. Her segues are so creative on stage, but they don't work out in print. You're not with her rhythm and that communal flow. There was much more material inside her than any of those lectures would have suggested in terms of a sustained thought pattern on those subjects." Finally, Marianne wrote an eighty-page book proposal.

In May 1988 Lowman submitted the proposal to eight publishers. "I was representing something that was sacred; it was important and required a publisher who would understand its meaning in the same way I did," he says. "I had chosen those editors and publishers quite carefully. Marianne came to town during one of her lecture visits and saw most of them. When I have an important book, I usually auction it. In an auction, the highest bidder usually gets the book, money being only a symbol of energy. Money is usually the deciding factor in those situations, but this time I decided I wanted to do it a little differently."

Instead of a straightforward auction, Lowman set up a "best offer blind option," in which the offers would be evaluated not only on the basis of money offered, but on a complete publishing program. "It was like holding gold," Lowman says of the project, "and you don't want the gold to be tarnished in any way. It should not be put into the wrong hands. It didn't seem she should be on the auction block as a property."

Lowman was known for his small but exclusive client list, and his submission letter made no bones about his enthusiasm for the Williamson project. "The first sentence of the submission letter was something like, 'This is one of the most important books I will ever sell,' and I went on to write that this lady and her materials had personally changed my life. It was an awesome letter, written straight from the heart, and that also added to the value."

Half the publishers put an offer on the table by the noon deadline for the sale. Just before the deadline Bill Shinker, then head of Harper & Row (now HarperCollins), phoned in "by far the most extraordinary bid for the book, as well as the most extraordinarily detailed publishing program," says Lowman. "I later found out that the reason he called in so late was because of the time zone difference. His San Francisco office, spurred by the secretary to the chairman, had called Bill and said, 'Get this book for whatever it takes. She's the hottest thing here on the West Coast.' It was a *magical* moment."

The book was sold in May 1988. Andrea Cagin, author of a successful book on the psychic surgeons of the Philippines, entitled *Awakening the Healer Within* worked with Marianne in the editing of the book.

Cagin had met Marianne in 1987 through a friend who was active in the AIDS community and was himself dying of AIDS. He had attended Marianne's lectures and had even performed funeral services with her. When her friend died, Cagin was unable to attend the funeral service. She asked Marianne for help and the two prayed together.

"It was a very intricate process," says Cagin, who worked for a year on what was originally thought to be a three-month project. "We worked side by side throughout. She would write something, and I would go over every sentence with her and say 'This works, this doesn't connect.' She has an ability to get information that just pours out, but one paragraph wasn't always connected to the next. So my job was to ensure all the sentences made sense and that everything flowed. We took apart and rearranged those eighty or so pages she had already completed. She's a perfectionist; she'd go over it many times, and sometimes we drove each other crazy. She works in a tremendous amount of maelstrom. Phone calls are coming in, the baby jumps on her in the middle of everything. So there's no time to have everything quiet—no phone calls, no interruptions. I never get a chance like that to work with her. Ever. Her life is not set up that way. She works in fits and starts. She's out of the room, she's in the room, she's eating something—it's her personality. So I had to adapt to that."

When Marianne was in Los Angeles, she and Cagin worked daily from approximately noon or one P.M. until five or six P.M. "You never wonder how Marianne's feeling that day," Cagin says with a smile. "You go in and there it is, she's either feeling great or like shit. It's hard to deal with full-throttle intensity all the time. A lot of people get frightened of it. When she's happy, she's happy. When she's angry, she's angry. You have to be in your own center around her. She's got a lot of seductive energy—not in a sexual way. Her energy is so strong that it's easy to fall into her wavelength and start moving with it. I learned early on that it would blow me out because I can't function the way she functions, and it wouldn't work if we both functioned the same way. I

just need to be myself. I would stay where I was an
she would stay where she was and we found a ba
ance.

"She's so incredibly loyal," Cagin adds. "Thi
morning I was upset, so I called Marianne and said
'You've got to do a prayer for me.' She said 'Okay
and stopped what she was doing to do a prayer fo
me on the phone. She would do anything for me.'"

Cagin, who is presently working with Marianne o
her next two books, describes their relationship a
"extremely harmonious. She would say 'I don't agre
with that,' and she might snap at me a little bit, an
I would say 'then leave it the way it is,' and tha
would be the end of it. She never lost her tempe
with me. She would get frustrated and so would
But we weren't afraid of that. She never holds on t
anything. She gets upset and then it's gone in on
minute. She does have a short fuse, and so do I,
Cagin admits, "but my fuse is longer than her
She's a very dynamic person, a generator. Sh
comes up with ideas and sparks the fire. In the mid
dle of writing the book, she was also serving on th
board of directors of the two centers. She had Proj
ect Angel Food, and she was doing these art auc
tions. She was doing too much, in my opinion. It'
almost like she's driven to do these things. Thes
ideas come and she's got to follow them. She neve
puts on the brakes. She's full speed ahead all th
time. I've never seen another human being functio
quite like that unless they're on drugs," Cagin says
laughing, "but she lives very healthily."

CHAPTER TEN

DOWN TO EARTH

During a question-and-answer session following a 1991 lecture in her hometown of Houston, a woman asked Marianne if she would still be accessible to her old friends even after she became a celebrity. "The question is," Marianne answered, "will *you* still like *me?*"

Marianne Williamson was now a celebrity, by definition fair game for critics and naysayers. In the spring of that year, a political dispute within the New York Center for Living board hit crisis level with the resignation of a key staff officer, Cynthia O'Neal, who took important fund-raising friends with her, including director Mike Nichols. Marianne ultimately asked the entire board to resign in order to make a fresh start. The incident left bruises and bitterness; sadly, much the same experience was to be repeated in Los Angeles.

In September 1991 Marianne and the staff of her Los Angeles Center for Living, along with high-powered friends, produced a huge, lavish charity event, an auction called "Divine Design." A large celebrity-filled crowd bid on such items as the corset Madonna wore on her "Blonde Ambition" tour, Arnold Schwarzenegger's leather jacket from *Terminator 2*, and an afternoon at Michael Jackson's ranch for a gaggle of lucky children. The event raised $750,000. But even as the accolades poured in, problems within the organization of the Los Angeles center were brewing. They would eventually culminate in Marianne's resignation from the board.

On February 16, 1992, the *Los Angeles Times* published a cover story on Marianne detailing the problems at the Centers for Living and relying for sources mainly on disgruntled associates—many of them unnamed—who accused Marianne of mismanagement, a lust for power, and an ungovernable temper. The article describes a fund-raiser for the Family Assistance Program in which Marianne waited for two hours on an auction block dressed in a strapless evening gown, spike heels, and wearing feathers in her hair, until the highest bidder, a man from the Midwest, forked up twelve hundred dollars to take her out for a night on the town. The article reports that Marianne told the co-auctioneer, talk show host Cyndy Garvey, to inform the crowd that she's "very interesting." Even Marianne's effort to help Patricia Shelhammer's charity was being viewed with a "journalistically" jaundiced eye.

People soon took up the rake to dredge up more muck. Like the *L.A. Times*, the feature article acknowledged grudgingly her remarkable charity work, but it also attacked Marianne's character, again largely based on misinformation and quotes from anonymous associates.

The *People* article opens with a dramatic scenario lifted from Divine Design, for which a hangar at Santa Monica airport had been transformed into a star-studded charity auction for Project Angel Food. Marianne delivers a speech on "love and forgiveness to rapt audience," but as she pushes her way toward the back of the audience, "barking" her apologies, she reveals what the writer implies is her true character:

> "What was that?" she hisses, launching a tirade at her audio-visual crew. "I told you!" The evening's slide presentation, a depiction of seriously ill AIDS patients, was, it seems, not "uplifting" enough.

The article cites low profits for the event, and places the blame on "questionable" amenities, such as air-conditioning, on Marianne's demanding and extravagant nature. According to *People*, Marianne fired the Manhattan Center for Living board, including Mike Nichols (who never served on that board), after which Nichols went on to create a rival AIDS support organization with Cynthia O'Neal and the executive director, Regina Hoover, whom Marianne supposedly dismissed in an act of unprecedented callousness. Hoover was put on probation, the article claims, just before surgery and chemotherapy treatments for her breast cancer, and then fired immediately before she was to undergo a bone marrow transplant.

None of these accusatory "facts" are true.

At the Los Angeles Center for Living, the article continues:

> The twenty member staff rebelled [in February] after the firing of the center's fourth director in five years, popular local politician Steve Schulte, who had clashed frequently with Williamson over business strategy. Some employees are attempting to unionize —in an effort, they say, to protect themselves from Williamson's bad-tempered caprices.

Since the critical cover story in the February 16, 1992, *Los Angeles Times, People* also stated, "at least one individual donor and one corporate donor say they have suspended financial contributions, and several demoralized Project Angel Food volunteers had to be dissuaded from resigning." Marianne had given her staff orders, *People* charged, "not to speak to reporters. Her words, according to witnesses: 'You're fucking with my livelihood, I'm famous—I don't need this, damn it!' "

Why the sudden media feeding frenzy on a woman who preaches love and service and who without any financial reward to herself had accomplished an extraordinary amount of good for the two largest cities in the United States? Why these distorted accounts when interviews with the actual parties concerned would have clearly revealed very different stories of what happened in both the New York and the Los Angeles Centers for Living? Why was Marianne being knocked off a pedestal she had always refused to mount?

Lynda Obst has described the press as a "heat-seeking unit, an infrared machine. If there are five people who have horrible things to say about you, that's who they'll talk to." This is certainly true, but there were other factors at work as well.

To a certain degree, the conflicts and changes of personnel within both Centers for Living can be attributed to the normal growing pains of any grass-roots organization that suddenly finds itself expanding beyond all initial expectations. As the founder and president of both boards, and the inspiration for the overwhelming majority of the volunteers, Marianne was the figurehead representing the Centers for Living. Whether or not she was directly involved in a particular conflict, the buck stopped with her. However, the vitriolic nature of some of the attacks cannot be explained by mere organizational "growing pains."

Like the "blueprints" engraved in seeds suggesting the likely fate of a plant, man's myths and archetypes contain the outlines of basic patterns of human behavior. Slaying the messenger seems to be one of mankind's favorite blood sports. Dionysus the Liberator was torn apart by the very people whom he inspired. And as noted in an earlier chapter, Prometheus suffered cruelly for his altruistic impulse. Both myths dramatize the high cost often paid for unselfish generosity. That's just the way it is, they tell us, and the backlash these myths describe often comes as a nasty, subversive rebellion. This is particularly true for a determined character such as Marianne Williamson, a fervent fighter for truth who cannot overlook a single wrong—particularly injustice against the underdog—and who sometimes can be brutally direct in her attempt to right that wrong. Simply by being herself—and Marianne Williamson is always herself—she invites challenge and confrontation from undermining forces.

"Marianne has an aspect which, on one level, is pretty inconsistent with who she is," says her longtime friend Andrea McDermott. "Historically, certain people have tried to humble her. They see that chin, that daunting walk, and they take it as a challenge to humble her. It happened now and then with certain people long before she became famous. It baffles her because she's coming from such an ingenuous place. She doesn't feel dauntless; she's really so sensitive and vulnerable."

Preaching a message of love and unity can be dangerous business, it seems. And if you refuse, like Marianne, to claim personal spiritual perfection, it becomes even more dangerous. Marianne used examples in her lectures of her own mistakes and stressed her role as costudent, a mere half step, at the most, ahead of her audience. She refused "followers" and welcomed "spiritual companions," yet the projected need for "guru" or "prophet," for an object of worship—someone to assume the burden of our own self-realization who can then be pilloried for it—was stronger, it seems, even than her frequent disclaimers.

Howard Rochestrie, who has experience in the nonprofit sector, blames part of the backlash criticism on the "big egos [that are] involved when people are doing things not for money. When they don't get the financial acknowledgment," he explains, "some people need the recognition in other ways."

"I think most of us, if we are honest with ourselves, realize that it would be a miracle to be as open-minded as we'd like to be," says Marianne. "Those of us in the spiritual community have to be on guard because the ego will use spiritual material as well as anything else. Look at all the consciousness bullies out there, 'I'm better than you because I'm a spiritual seeker' or 'I'm different than you because I'm a spiritual seeker' or 'My spiritual seeking is better than yours' or 'You should be doing spiritual seeking.' "

Finally, it must be noted that behavior praised as assertive and decisive in men is often condemned as strident and bitchy in women, particularly if the woman in question is young, beautiful, fashionable, and candid, as is Marianne Williamson.

The first whiff of troubles brewing at Marianne's charities was picked up by the press at the second annual Fantasy Auction held in March 1991 at Sotheby's in Manhattan, to raise funds for the New York Center for Living. Mike Nichols led the evening off by bidding twelve thousand dollars for "a portrait of your pet by William Wegman." The offerings on the block—a portrait of your children by Richard Avedon, a job as an extra in a Woody Allen movie, dinner with Harrison Ford, various dates with Lauren Bacall, Steve Martin, Liza Minelli, and Robin Williams—were geared to affluent, artsy Manhattanites. Dressed in tight black pants, gold boots, and a chartreuse silk tunic, Marianne spent the evening standing quietly at the back of the room, reported *Vanity Fair* magazine, which also noted that a controversy was brewing among board members over the issue of prayer. Marianne had been told that if she invoked God's name during her speech of greeting, "checkbooks would snap shut." She made do, the article reports, with a passing mention of "vibrations of love and understanding" and a single, hurried, "We bless all of you and ask that you all join with us in blessing God."

"The press made that more than it was," Marianne says today. "But it was symbolic of a real problem in that my spiritual input was not appreciated by pretty much the entire board." Speaking of the volunteers working at the center who were largely drawn from her *Course in Miracles* lecture audience, she wonders, "Who do you think the volunteers [for the Centers for Living] were?"

David Geffen told *Vanity Fair:*

It's easy to make fun of people who are coming from a spiritual place. It's very New Age, and that's reason enough for a lot of people to snicker. I think people are generally suspicious of anyone who is involved in

spiritual causes, but there's no question
Marianne is genuine, and she does a lot of
good work. She's not some new version of Aimee Semple McPherson. She doesn't hold
herself out to be a perfect person, but she
takes care of people who are in trouble and
who are dying. She's also able to articulate
things that are valuable for people to hear.
People are alienated from their families, from
religion, and she's found a way to bring them
together. She's not a saint, but she does as-
pire to do good work and to inspire other
people to do good work. This is her calling;
she decided to do this. I'm pretty cynical, but
I'm incredibly moved by what she does.

Psychologist Pat Buckley came on the board for
the New York Center for Living "by default," she
says, when "they found out that another Ph.D./psy-
chologist on the board didn't believe in God." As
Marianne stood by, Buckley handed her peer a pamphlet on the psychotherapeutic aspects of *A Course
in Miracles.*

"What's all this God stuff?" the board member ex-
claimed.

"It's okay in the Center to say God and to pray and
to say whatever you want," Marianne replied.

"The psychologist became upset," Buckley recalls,
"and I happened to be standing there. Marianne
asked if I would take over."

Buckley continues:

It soon became apparent that there were two perspectives: ego and *Course in Miracles*–based. Those two approaches therefore led to two different effects and perceptions. I remember saying to someone—I don't remember if they were on the board or if it was the center director—"This is the perspective of the *Course of Miracles*" in reference to something I was doing at the center. "Well, this is not *A Course in Miracles Center*," they replied. And I said, "I thought it wás. That's news to me." It became a dualistic situation that resulted naturally in conflict, unnecessary but necessary because it can be a learning experience . . .

Marianne and I had prayed many times over the phone. Being on the board, we had many opportunities to pray. Marianne is very accessible to healing and to being there. She's willing to participate in the healing process both in business and personal life.

The hostilities came to a head, not over the issue of God's presence in the Center for Living, but over a conflict between executive director Regina Hoover and program director Cynthia O'Neal, whose fundraising efforts and long-standing friendships with such people as Mike Nichols and Stephen Sondheim had greatly benefited the center. O'Neal was erroneously tagged by some reporters as the main opponent to prayer at the Sotheby auction, an unlikely prospect given her longtime participation in healing prayer circles.

For O'Neal, problems within the center began when Marianne determined that staff members could not also serve on the board. Since O'Neal was program director, she resigned from the board, but she marks that decision as the beginning of a division between staff and board members. After it was determined that the business end of the center could be run more efficiently, Regina Hoover was hired as executive director in October 1990. "It quickly seemed clear to me that she didn't really understand what we were doing there," O'Neal says today. "Also, changes began happening . . . sort of in the name of this is the proper way to do things."

O'Neal had been at the center from its very beginnings. She says:

> When I saw things were going way off the mark, I would address it, and my remarks were met with a good deal of crossness. I finally found myself getting there at seven in the morning, just to be alone.
>
> One day, a call came at four o'clock in the afternoon. A kid was in the hospital, alone in his room. The doctor had just left his room after giving him a bombshell of a lab report. He had no family, no one, he hadn't lived in New York long, and he was sobbing on the phone. I said, "I'll be right there." An appropriate reaction, I would think, given what we were doing. But later I was told I wasn't be-

ing paid to make hospital visits. That began to be the tone of it, bureaucratic. Regina Hoover perceived me as an enemy, as I was a stumbling block for her, so she had to get me out of there to do what she wanted to do, to take it over and run it the way she wanted.

I was told by Marianne and the board that we had to support Regina Hoover, that she was the executive director and she had to be allowed to run things. Mind you, at this point there were many board members who were appalled, who thought it was the most enormous mistake and what we needed to do was fix it right then. We needed to say, "Thank you, we're so sorry." But that did not happen.

One morning, O'Neal discovered a memo Hoover had left on her desk: "It was rather in the tone of something you might have found in your gym locker in high school if you had gone out with another girl's boyfriend. She wrote that I was ruining the place with my vicious undermining of her efforts and I had to stop my disgusting badmouthing of Marianne. There wasn't a true sentence in it." The memo also notified O'Neal that "in light of the above," she was on probation. "It was actually wonderful," O'Neal says with an ironic smile, "because I didn't have to wrestle with it. I thought, 'Probation? I don't think so.'"

A second memo had gone to other staff members, "telling them they were not allowed to speak to me unless she was present." O'Neal immediately Xerox copied the two memos and sent them with a letter of resignation to Marianne and all the board members. "I didn't have to say anything. I just said, 'Thank you, blah, blah, it's been the most thrilling three years,' which was absolutely true. While there was a lot of relief, because I knew I wasn't going to have to get up one more morning of my life and drag myself in to work in such an hysterical, tense atmosphere, I was heartbroken about the clients, all my pals I'd been with for three years."

A few days after O'Neal handed in a copy of the memos and her resignation, she heard from Marianne, who wanted to know if there was any possibility of a healing between O'Neal and Hoover. O'Neal said no. O'Neal asked to continue facilitating the Wednesday night AIDS support group that Marianne ran once or twice a month when she was in town. Marianne agreed.

Some members of the board resigned over the issue—journalist Jean Halberstram, Paul Werner, and, some time later, chiropractor Alan Pressman. Mike Nichols, who had served on the advisory board and helped the center with fund-raisers such as the Fantasy Auction, withdrew his support. Some clients and others wrote letters supporting O'Neal.

"I really didn't know what I was going to do," says O'Neal. "The next morning, I was sitting at my desk in a slight state of shock, and the phone rang. It was Mike Nichols, just checking in. 'How's everything, how's it going?' he asked. 'Funny you should ask,' I said. 'Listen to something.' I read him the two memos, and he instantly said, 'Well, fuck them, we'll raise the money and do another place.' But I couldn't think of it in that moment; I just ran right past it."

Not too long after she left the Center for Living, O'Neal did start another AIDS support organization with Nichols's help and that of John Juska, another former staff member from the Manhattan Center for Living. Ironically, a few weeks after O'Neal's departure, Hoover discovered she had breast cancer, and eventually left the center herself.

Ellie Ellsworth, a close friend to both Marianne and Cynthia O'Neal, often found herself on the telephone with both women, attempting to mediate the situation:

It was difficult for them both. Since I wasn't really privy to exactly what went on, I'm only an outsider with an opinion. So I don't really want to offer one. I know Marianne gets very fearful and afraid around organizations, that's something she really needs to work on, I think. I know she will. The point is that she started this center that has a profound effect on people. I once came to Cynthia O'Neal when I was really upset about something that wasn't about Marianne but I was able to turn it into something about Marianne. Cynthia said to me, "Never confuse the messenger with the message." I've heard that before, but at that moment it hit me between the eyes. That's been my philosophy about Marianne. Do not confuse the message with the messenger. The messenger may be all apart or may be needing help or support or love, but the message is pure and it comes through her. That's clear to me. Why is Marianne the likely messenger? Probably because of something Silver Friedman [who with her husband Bud created the Improv comedy club] said to me. I had asked her, "Silver, why is comedy so successful? My cabaret world isn't as successful as that. Why?" She said, "Because the comedians speak of what's in our minds, and we wish we could stand up and speak the way they speak." That's how Marianne is.

The dissension on the board over "prayer" and the "Hoover–O'Neal" issues became so great that Marianne finally decided to ask the board to resign in order that a new start be made. One of those who left the board was Bruce Bierman. He maintains that "it was a very important thing for her to do.

"The board was not working cohesively, and a lot of it had to do with problems with Regina," Bierman acknowleges. "Regina had cancer, and Marianne refused to fire her. "No one wanted Cynthia to resign, but an organization can't be blackmailed and say 'We'll hire someone else.' The memos were outrageous, but you don't know what went on from the other side. We tried to patch things up between Cynthia and Regina. I wish that things would have worked out a little easier, but bottom line is that we're serving the community. People are being helped, and we're talking about a situation that involves a handful of people coloring the work that serves hundreds of people every week."

According to Bierman, some board members wanted to fire Hoover:

My personal feeling is that there were things on which Regina did a great job and things that I was not as happy as I might have been, in terms of personal communication with her staff. But Regina was very instrumental in getting a lot of the women's groups at the center. The point is that the *People* magazine article incorrectly implied that Marianne had fired the board and then fired the director.

That was not my take on it. I remember Marianne saying, "This woman has breast cancer. We're an organization that deals with people with life-challenging illnesses. She's going in for a double mastectomy in two weeks. How can you do this?" I remember Marianne saying to me afterward, "This is an unworkable situation. I cannot work with people who would treat others this way." I thought, "Right on." I felt the same way, that you don't treat people that way. I didn't want to fire Regina then, not based on the information. I was unhappy with her, but I don't know what I would have done. But the board's vote was split and she wasn't fired.

If Marianne was controlling, as some press reports suggest, she would have jumped in and done it her way. Marianne has a vision, but no one wants to be a follower anymore. Everyone wants to be a leader.

Bierman was asked to join the new board. Though he remains very involved with the center, he refused, feeling "it was more important that Marianne be given an opportunity to start with a clean slate, with a new board."

Charles Young was asked to join the new board in August 1991, after Hoover took a leave of absence due to illness. Only one other member was on the board at this time, professional accountant Bob Halfon, who was taking care of the organization's financial concerns. Together with Marianne, they worked on "restoring a sense of equilibrium and serenity to the organization and fund-raising," says Young, "a big issue because with the departure of a number of people because of this Cynthia-Regina thing, the ability of the center to raise money had been impaired." Despite diminishing funds, "the center continued Regina's salary and contributed to her support as long as they possibly could, until they encountered financial difficulties at the end of the year. They were in severe financial trouble, and a donation was made to give her a generous severance payment, with the agreement that obviously we would help her in any way we could to find something new and also to continue her insurance through most of the next year. In fact, Marianne and

I were the two people who worked with Regina. Even though the center did not have much money and she had worked there for only a year, it continued her on the payroll at her full salary for six months after she had stopped working there."

Meanwhile, on the West Coast, plans were being made for Divine Design, a Los Angeles center/Project Angel Food fund-raiser, which was set to happen around the same time that Marianne's finished manuscript was due to be delivered to HarperCollins. When no one volunteered to produce the fund-raiser, Marianne took charge.

Marianne's apartment became a beehive of activity from early morning until one or two in the morning, taken over by a swarm of volunteers, ringing telephones, and pizza deliveries. Amid calls to get people to come to the fund-raiser, interviews with the media, officiating at funerals and weddings, flying to New York every month, facilitating her weekly AIDS support group, lecturing in Los Angeles three times a week, counseling, running both Centers for Living, and raising her toddler, Marianne managed to steal a few hours each day to finish *A Return to Love*, working with Andrea Cagin in her bedroom. Yet some volunteers looked upon their service as a golden opportunity to get counseling on private problems from Marianne Williamson, a fair trade, they thought, for their efforts. If she refused, pleading lack of time, they would become angry and secretly malign her.

"People at the center were scapegoating her," says Rich Cooper. "They wouldn't talk to her. They wouldn't return the phone calls. They were down on her. I don't know why. It is mind-boggling to me. When she first started the center, she sort of kept her hands off, and she was criticized because she wasn't there a lot. But when she was there, they criticized her for being there too much."

"Marianne had no reason to give so much to the gay community except that was the community she decided to serve because it was so devastated by AIDS," says David Kessler, who is now president of the Los Angeles board.

Divine Design was a great success. Victoria Pearman worked in the designer's boutique at Divine Design. "I thought that event was amazing," she says. Bette Midler and Sandy Gallin opened the show, Los Angeles's best-known designers created rooms, and designer fashions sold for a fraction of their cost. "God knows there's a recession going on, and she still raised that money [$750,000]. And it was fun. All my friends came and they had a blast."

Linda Ford, who handled public relations for the event, recalls Marianne telling the staff that she would appreciate it if they'd take up any issues with her and not the media. "She never ordered anybody not to talk to media," Ford protests. *People* also reported Divine Design's goal was to take in two million dollars. ."The goal was to make one million," says Ford, "and the event grossed one point two million. They netted $750,000. So it was very successful, and for more than one reason. Here we were in the middle of the worst recession in over a decade, with charities getting hurt left and right, and they still netted three quarter of a million dollars."

Another criticism leveled by *People* was that Marianne ordered air-conditioning for the airport hangar. No mention was made in the article of the fact that the indoor temperature was ninety-five degrees. Some of those present had paid as much as ten thousand dollars a person to attend the event, and the year before, Marvin Davis's wife, Barbara, had walked out of Angel Art because the gallery was overcrowded and swelteringly hot. "The air-conditioning was essential, it would have hurt the event more to not have had it," Ford asserts. "Marianne was the only one with the brains and the guts to say 'This is what we have to have.' "

The Los Angeles Center for Living had already gone through three executive directors and one change of locale by the time Divine Design took place. The first director, Stuart Altschuler, was fired by Marianne. The second, Heath Hanner, left because she relocated. After being hired in October 1990, Dick de Vogeleare was fired from the by-now $60,000 a year post in April 1991, but not by Marianne. "I was not the one who got rid of him," she says. "Many two-faced people in this group."

"What's not known a lot is that Dick de Vogeleare was on the board," explains David Kessler. "We were interviewing for the executive director but we couldn't find anyone. 'I could do this,' Dick said. When he got into the job, there were a lot of areas that needed attention, for which he didn't bring forth the experience and know-how. I think he was a wonderful guy and his heart was truly in the right place. It was the board that decided to make the change. He was friends with Marianne and it was very hard on her. It was painful for both of them.

"It is hard for any of us to come to our limits," Kessler adds. "To be the executive director, you have to do a wide range of things; an organization can't change itself to meet the needs of the individuals who are working there. We have to do what's best for the community and the organization as a whole."

Unlike Stuart Altschuler, de Vogeleare criticized Marianne to the press, which further exacerbated the situation.

"A lot of people don't realize that Marianne, like anyone else, was a volunteer who was giving forty to sixty hours a week," Kessler continues. "To be criticized the way she was—even by brand-new staff members—when she had given her blood, money, and time was a bit of a setup."

De Vogeleare and Marianne are no longer friends, and de Vogeleare still evidences mixed feelings regarding her. "After I had spoken to the reporter for the *L.A. Times*, Marianne got extremely virulent with me," he says. "She wouldn't even listen to what I'd said. The reporter was stupid: I had said a lot of wonderful things about Marianne, and I also mentioned incidences because of my experience of being fired from the position of director of the L.A. Center for Living. Unfortunately, the *Times* didn't quote me on those positive things I'd said. They just picked up the negative comments."

After allowing a cooling-off period to pass, de

Vogeleare sent Marianne a card. "We have a lot of good history here; let's try to repair the pieces," he wrote. There was no response. De Vogeleare then assisted Dan Stone in producing Marianne's 1992 Easter lecture, a beautifully choreographed pageant held at a cathedral-sized church in the mid-Wilshire section of Los Angeles, which also featured musicians, singers, and towering floral arrangements. After the service, de Vogeleare felt moved to telephone Marianne because of what he describes as her attacking behavior backstage toward some volunteers:

> I said very nicely, "Marianne, I got a wake-up call this morning at five o'clock to be at the theater at seven to put on an event for you. And from the moment you got there, all you did was complain. I find your behavior to be just deplorable." Well, within moments she was calling me back, screaming at me on the phone, "Dick, you're causing me too many problems. Do me a favor: never, ever call me again," and then she hung up on me. So that's where the relationship is at the moment.

De Vogeleare also speaks at length and with enthusiasm on Marianne's tremendous compassion, generosity, and visionary gifts, and maintains that "at some point I would like to have a relationship with her. But everything changed when I went to work for her. It was fine up till then. This is pure conjecture on my part, but when I became the director for the Los Angeles Center for Living—I was the third one—I think as president of the board she thought she could control me and tell me how to do my job. I was having some problems with some other members of the board too, but it wasn't my fault that the center was in a financial crunch; that was something they did wrong.

"I had been kind of warned about becoming an employee," de Vogeleare continues, "but I really wanted to leave the job I had. I had just turned fifty, and I thought, 'This is a great time for a mid-life change.' My heart and soul were really there at the center. When I was fired, I felt Marianne betrayed me. I think she could have stood up for me, and she didn't. I could be wrong, but that's what I think, only because of what I've been told."

"I don't know what some people want from her," says a person who works closely with Marianne. "The stuff they pin on her they wouldn't on others in their lives. It's like 'Mommy wasn't nice to me.'"

Steve Schulte, a popular figure who had once served as West Hollywood's mayor, became the fourth director of the Los Angeles Center for Living. "He was brought in on a temporary basis," states David Kessler. "And Steve made it clear that this was not a job that he wanted forever and that he would be moving on at some point."

After nine or ten months, "the board, not just Marianne, felt it was time," Kessler says, although widespread reports in the press spoke of a conflict similar to that within the New York Center over spiritual orientation. Attacks against Marianne escalated with Schulte's firing, and there was talk about unionizing the Los Angeles Center for Living staff.

Before a fifth director could be found, David Kessler ran the center until he was able to bring in Steve Bennett, a former executive director of AIDS Project Los Angeles, for a ninety-day period only. As of this writing, William Wells, hired from Children's Hospital Foundation, has taken over the position.

Marianne was reported in the *L.A. Times* and other publications to have fired her entire Los Angeles board. In fact, it was Kessler who suggested a more efficient dual board system, one comprised of those interested in fund-raising, the other of those more concerned with the day-to-day activities of the center. "When you had those two groups on one board," Kessler explains, "it didn't always work well, because when you discuss, 'Should we buy a new copier machine?' the fund-raising people are bored, and when you discuss fund-raising, the business people are bored."

The three men reportedly fired from the board by Marianne—Waldo Fernandez; Michael Childers, from whom Marianne is estranged because of disparaging remarks he made to the press; and Howard Rosenman, with whom she is mending a relationship—were actually moved to the fund-raising board. "They all said it sounded fine and it made a lot of sense," says Kessler. "Sandy Scott became involved with her own church and didn't have the time, so she resigned"—only to step back on a temporary basis to help out—"and Louise Hays moved out of town."

Many of Marianne's friends and coworkers wrote to the *Los Angeles Times* and *People* magazine to protest the unfair treatment of her in their articles and to correct the errors in reporting, but neither publication saw fit to publish any of those letters in the "Letters to the Editor" section. David Kessler and other board members wrote the following to the *Los Angeles Times* and *People:*

February 21, 1992
Letter to the Editor
LOS ANGELES TIMES
Times Mirror Square
Los Angeles, CA 90053

Dear *Los Angeles Times* Editor,

With regard to your cover story in the Calendar section, "The Power, the Glory, the Glitz," an article about Marianne Williamson written by Terry Pristin, I do feel a need to point out a few corrections. As the President of the Board of the Los Angeles Center for Living, I feel very strongly about some of the misinformation in the article.

First of all it is absolutely incorrect that "Williamson purged her Los Angeles Board of Rosenman, Childers, (and) Fernandez." When discussions started around me becoming President, one of the things that I felt was not working at the Center was a mixture of people with different interests and talents on one Board and I am the one who made the suggestion to reorganize the Board according to people's talents and form two separate Boards. Those whose areas of expertise were in administration, i.e., business owners or those with financial backgrounds, would be on the Board of Directors and they would be responsible for the overall running of the Center in the day-in/day-out as well as its longterm effectiveness. Those whose talents and clout were in the area of fund-raising, major gifts, and capital campaigns would be on our Fund-raising Board; hence one Board was divided into two.

Howard Rosenman, Michael Childers, and Waldo Fernandez are extremely important friends of the Los Angeles Center For Living/ Project Angel Food who have brought their incredible talents to help us in many areas. Since this reorganization of the Board, all members have been in touch with the Center and remain vital forces in its continual growth and still exercise an enormous commitment to people who are facing life-challenging illnesses and AIDS.

I'm extremely worried when I read statements such as Ms. Pristin's. These gifted men give not only their talents, but their time, to an organization, and then something so inaccurate is printed regarding them.

Secondly, it is incorrect that I "run a nursing home for AIDS patients." I have a home health agency that specializes in providing in-home nursing care for people with AIDS; my agency's service area is Los Angeles County.

In terms of the overall Center for Living, no one likes changes; but sometimes in extreme growth they become necessary.

We as an organization and as a Board feel very lucky to have someone such as Marianne Williamson, who not only founded this agency, which helps hundreds of people per day, but continues to be its guiding vision, quality control, and our main fund-raiser (there are very few people in this town who can compare with Marianne Williamson's fund-raising abilities). Besides all that, she continues to have weekly contact with the clients, those people with AIDS and other life-challenging illnesses directly affected by the Center and what it does. Marianne continues to meet with them in a weekly group to lend her own unique support session to people with AIDS.

We at the Los Angeles Center for Living want to thank you for the coverage you have given us. As with any media coverage, it will always, hopefully, bring in more volunteers and more supporters who will allow us to better serve our clients and people with AIDS and to provide more meals.

Sincerely,

DAVID KESSLER,

President

March 17, 1992

PEOPLE MAGAZINE

Time & Life Building

Rockefeller Center

New York, N.Y. 10020

To the Editor:

We feel compelled to write to you to set forth some truths regarding misstatements and misrepresentations which appeared in your article about Marianne Williamson and the Los Angeles Center for Living, entitled "The Divine Ms. W." The article contains numerous defamatory statements apparently published in reckless disregard for the truth or with actual knowledge of falsity for the purpose of injuring Ms. Williamson's and the Center's reputations. Among the defamatory statements are the following:

1. "Not long before that story's publication, Williamson warned her staff not to speak to reporters." That statement is false and defamatory, and infers [sic] that Ms. Williamson threatened the staff. Neither she nor any other Board member would suggest that any staff member conceal information. The

statement refers to a request Ms. Williamson made of the staff to speak directly with her about their issues rather than speaking to the press.

2. "Among the developments that have most rankled insiders were the disappointing profits of the Divine Design auction expected to generate something like $2 million, it netted only $725,000. The reason, say her critics, was Williamson's micromanagement of the event. Potential profits were eaten away, they say by Williamson's insistence on such questionable amenities as air conditioning for the hangar." These statements, once again, are false and defamatory. The auction was never expected to generate $2 million in profits. Moreover, there is no basis for your article's assertion that the auction would have netted another $1,275,000 but for "Williamson's micromanagement of the event." That is simply not true. It is also not true that air-conditioning the hangar—when temperatures were in the 90's in Los Angeles —ate away profits through "questionable amenities." Indeed, in light of the reality of the recession facing this country, we were elated and amazed that the auction proved such a success. Your article showed such a complete disregard for what was achieved, that even were it not false and defamatory, your intent was shameful.

3. "It may simply be that in the case of Marianne Williamson, as with other cult figures before her, private life does not—and cannot —match public expectation." The reference to Ms. Williamson as a "cult figure" is false and defamatory. Those who study the *Course in Miracles* or simply wish to attend her lectures are not part of a cult. In light of the tenor of the article, perhaps you intended to imply that those who suffer from AIDS, the HIV virus, or other serious diseases, or are clients of the Center, are part of a cult, since that is the community that receives most of Ms. Williamson's attention. If that be the case, the absence of any ethical responsiblity in your writing is profound and disturbing.

4. "She's using it to self-promote." This is simply not true. Ms. Williamson has never used the Center for self-promotion. In fact, as her popularity in the press has grown, we have been grateful that she has included the Center in such a prominent fashion. It has raised our visibility in a way that would be impossible, or at least very difficult, to attain on our own.

In closing, we would like to state that your clear disregard for the work of the Center and its benefit to the Los Angeles community is appalling. If we have lost a few supporters because of Ms. Williamson, it is eclipsed by the hundreds who have come forward because of her. To undermine her involvement at the Center is to undermine the Center itself, and the services we provide to thousands of people facing life-challenging illnesses. This is a time when responsible people should encourage involvement, growth, and giving, not degrade it.

The Board of Directors
The Los Angeles Center for Living

Hurt and discouraged by the vitriolic nature of these attacks and fearful of the negative effect it would have on the center's ability to fulfill its mission, Marianne stepped down from her position of president of the board of the Los Angeles Center for Living.

As of this writing, the board of development for the Los Angeles Center consists of Waldo Fernandez, Michael Childers, Howard Rosenman, Robert Harvey, Barry Karras, Barbara Foley, and Dan Stone. The board of business affairs consists of David Kessler, president; Edward Rada, CPA, treasurer; Melinda A. McIntyre; Ron Gelb, Ph.D.; Judy Spiegal, M.P.H.; Reverend Sandy Scott; Marck Locher; Ralph Hansen, M.D.; Vee Hart Mell, Pharm.D., J.D.; and Byron Tyler.

Charlotte Patton, who helps organize the New York lectures, recalls Marianne's fears that the *People* magazine article would adversely affect her ability to speak the message of *A Course in Miracles.* 'One night the weather was very bad and we didn't have a very good turnout," Patton recalls. "Mari anne said, 'Do you think it's because of the *Peopl* article?' "

"Can you imagine if you'd given six or seven year of your life, day and night, your time, your money your friends, your energy, your lectures?" Lind Ford questions rhetorically. "Ninety percent of th Project Angel Food volunteers came from her re quests for help at every lecture. She taught thes people how to be of service. For them to turn aroun and say, 'Okay, I've had enough.' How insulting How shortsighted! What are they going to do tw weeks from now when they don't have enough vo unteers on a Sunday? They can't call up Mariann and say, 'Can you make an announcement?' C course, she still would. That's the kind of perso she is."

"I had been given a warning very serendipitousl that the *L.A. Times* was out to screw me," Mariann says, "but I didn't listen. I didn't expect any meda from the mayor, but if someone asks is the city be ter in certain forms because I came here, then tha really says something about the press, that the would choose to do what they did. You get the fee ing with a lot of reporters that they are out to expos something, but the problem is, expose what? Peopl don't deserve what they do."

Was it strange to read about herself? "I never rea about *myself*," Marianne replies. "For the most par I've read about someone else. It's pathetic."

Marianne writes in *A Return to Love:* "The remova of ego is not the removal of personality. What we ca

Jesus' anger was energy. An outburst of emotion doesn't have to be so quickly labeled anger. It's a release of energy and doesn't have to be thought of as a negative or 'unspiritual' emotion."

In response to criticisms of her behavior cited in the *Times* article and *People* articles, Marianne says, "If they think it's not behavior worthy of Jesus, well, look again at Jesus. It's not behavior worthy of Mother Teresa? Well, look again at Mother Teresa. These people say, 'That's not loving behavior.' I stand by some of my behavior in that situation. Even the stories that are true, you say that wasn't loving? I say, 'It *was* loving.' I told Terry Pristin"—who wrote the *L.A. Times* piece—" 'If I had not behaved the way I did, then you would be writing an article about this organization [the L.A. Center for Living], that their administrative costs are up to "here" and their service is down to "there," they spend thousands of dollars on messenger services, blah blah.'

"By the way," Marianne adds, referring to a much-quoted comment she allegedly made, "I did not call myself 'a bitch for God.' I said, 'This image that some people have of me as a bitch for God is somewhat ironic.' "

"It's been very interesting since I've taken over as president," comments David Kessler. "I say the same things Marianne Williamson said, and people say, 'Oh! He's decisive, direct, and aggressive! He's a good leader!' Marianne says it, and they say, 'Who does she think she is?' Our society doesn't allow women to hold positions of power."

Kessler recently attended a gala dinner at the Biltmore Hotel in downtown Los Angeles honoring Sam Williamson for a lifetime's work on behalf of human rights. "They described Marianne's father as determined, persistent, and direct," Kessler recalls. "Marianne and I looked at each other, and I said, 'Those are all the qualities everyone thinks you shouldn't have!' They honor him for the very same qualities they criticize her!"

During her ordeal with the Centers for Living and the press, Marianne and *Murphy Brown* producer Gary Donzig talked about *A Course in Miracles* point of view on attack. The course teaches the importance of remaining defenseless. But, as Donzig notes, "your instinct is to immediately attack back. In the midst of being blasted in a public forum by mostly 'an unnamed source,' she was trying to extract the lesson. She really worked on herself. 'Okay,' she said, "some of these criticisms may really be valid and therefore I'm going to look at myself more clearly and say, 'If these are valid, what do I have to do about them?' That's what she said to me, and in one of her lectures, and even in one of those articles—that not everything was necessarily untrue, and those comments she found true . . . she was more than willing to work on. That impressed me enormously. The fact that she was big enough to actually open herself up."

"I know how much Marianne was hurt," says former board member Sandy Scott. "She said to me, 'Sandy, I'm just going to give up and step aside.' I said, 'Don't you dare, don't let them win! Don't let them gobble you.' But she said, 'I don't know.' I think they are childish and immature people who are projecting Mom and Dad. Now they're thinking, 'We've gotten rid of Marianne.' Well, the mirror is still there. Who's next? Probably the next director."

CHAPTER ELEVEN

NOT A GODDESS

By the end of 1991 Marianne faced a major cross-roads in her life. One avenue seemed to have been closed off to her, but another would soon open onto an arena where Marianne could play her ascensionist role on a broader and perhaps more profound scale.

All during the storm and stress of Divine Design, the rebellion within the Los Angeles center, and Marianne's negative press, HarperCollins had been readying *A Return to Love*, officially scheduled for publication on February 26, 1992.

On February 4, just before publication date and mere days before the negative *L.A. Times* and *People* articles hit newsstands, Marianne appeared on the *Oprah Winfrey* television talk show. Winfrey endorsed Marianne's book with unabashed hyperbole, telling millions of viewers that one reading of the book had produced 157 miracles in Winfrey's own life (after which she stopped counting). She then distributed one thousand copies to her studio audience. "Oprah got her book and went crazy over it," reports Andrea Cagin, who worked on *Return* alongside Marianne. "Nobody said 'Oprah push this.' Nobody tells Oprah to do anything. Oprah called her and said, 'I know you well from this book; let's do a show. This is the book I've been waiting for.' Marianne and I have always talked about breaking out the champagne," Cagin says with a laugh, "but as soon as it happened, which was about three days after the book was in stores, she was off on her book tour. She called me up the other day and said, 'We never celebrated.' I said 'I know.' We're going out to brunch on Sunday."

(Marianne would make a return visit to Winfrey's program in late June 1992, after that initial enthusiastic endorsement helped rocket *Return* to the number-one spot on the nation's nonfiction lists, a position it has held as of this writing for nineteen weeks.)

As Winfrey's viewers descended on bookstores demanding Marianne's book, its publication date was hastily pushed forward and hundreds of thousands more copies were printed. HarperCollins sent Marianne on an extensive cross-country book tour, which she sandwiched in between weekly trips to Los Angeles for AIDS support groups and Monday lectures at the Sheraton Miramar Hotel in Santa Monica and monthly stops in New York for her AIDS support group there and lectures at Town Hall.

"It all came in such a whirlwind," says Andrea Cagin, who had felt compelled to study the course and had completed the workbook only six months before she was asked to work with Marianne. "She was not expecting this. I knew it was going to be strong, but I didn't know it was going to hit number one in a week and stay there. You can't know it. I felt the energy when we were writing it. I knew it would be very important, but I didn't know how ready the world was, how needed it was, and that they would grab on to this book with so much caring, love, and desire. I've seen what she's done for the AIDS community in Los Angeles. I saw how people were taking to her because, while we were working, I observed her on a daily basis. She goes to hospitals and prays over people who are dying. I've seen the amount of support she has given and how appreciative people are. But I wasn't aware of this larger scale. I personally felt very proud because I worked on the book, but beyond that, I felt very heartened that people took to this material so well."

Al Lowman was on a business trip in Key West, Florida, when the *Oprah Winfrey* show aired. "Marianne had told me a week before what that show was going to be on. I knew that certain comments by Oprah Winfrey were going to be on the air, but I didn't know how dramatic that show was or what Oprah Winfrey's tone had been. As the program was into its first ten or fifteen minutes, Oprah said, 'I've never been as personally moved by any one book or author as this one.' I weeped. It was such validation for four years of incredible work. I knew what that was going to bring. I wasn't surprised by the book's impact, but I was surprised that it occurred that fast. Within three weeks there were 750,000 copies in print.

"To this day, I don't think Marianne has let that moment affect her," Lowman marvels. "She's always looking to 'How can I better myself?' I find a lot of creative people I work with to be that way. It's not that they're focusing on the negative, it's 'What could I have done better?' "

"When it was first published, I was hoping it would sell enough that I wouldn't be too embarrassed," Marianne admits.

"Now that it's been successful, I'm not surprised. People are attracted to a message of hope. I'm attracted to a message of hope. Their enthusiasm is simply mirroring my own."

During a stop on her book tour in Houston, proud parents Sophie Ann and Sam held an elaborate tea for their daughter. Marianne lectured at a local church and did a book-signing at the old Alabama Theater (now a bookstore), where she attended movies as a teenager. A long line of her readers filed past the marquee emblazoned with her name. "The idea of coming back as a star is an illusion," she told the *Houston Post*. "I'm doing the exact same thing I've been doing for quite a few years. More people know about it, but there's no change in what I do."

Marianne also reunited with high school friends, among them Cindy Freedman, herself a singer who currently hosts a Pacifica radio show for women in Houston. "They got together for a show," says Marianne's friend and former high school teacher, June Smith. "It was just wonderful to hear them laugh.

Cindy did a quick interview with Marianne, and it was like they were fifteen years ago. Cindy taped it and told me, 'I want you to hear this because it will remind you of many times we spent together.' "

Valerie Lippincot accompanied Marianne for parts of the book tour:

There'd be long lines of people and she'd always listen. They'd received so much inspiration from her book, and they had a couple of minutes to get some comfort or words of wisdom. She always made the time. The book-signing would be scheduled for an hour, but she would always go over the limit and talk privately to people or say, "Call me or call my office." I don't think every person would make themselves that available.

One mature woman was talking with Marianne—I don't know where we were—but she admired Marianne's necklace, which I knew Marianne had bought recently. Marianne said, "You like it? Here!" Here was this gorgeous necklace made of hearts, but that's the way Marianne is. And the way she does it also makes it casual, no big thing.

I remember when we were at the airport. We had stopped at a little muffin place. A man didn't have enough money and they didn't take credit cards, which he had. He didn't speak very much English, and she said, "I'll pay for it." It was just five bucks, but that's what she does. I remember once we were going to a party and we stopped to pick up some food. She saw somebody by a garbage can and she said, "Here, Val, give him this." It was forty bucks. When we walked around New York, she'd hand money to anyone who looked like they needed it.

After completing her tour of America, Marianne came to realize that, Oprah's endorsement notwithstanding, the book had been a success because of the "deep spiritual hunger" in America. "This is not a trend . . . there are a lot of people speaking about these things," she says. "I believe transformational speakers and writers will be to the nineties what musicians were to the sixties."

Marianne's audience had expanded beyond Los Angeles and Manhattan, beyond an audience dominated by the gay community, disaffected yuppies, Hollywoodites, and spiritual seekers, to penetrate the troubled heartland of America.

Katherine Harvey, who assists Marianne with her correspondence, recalls receiving a simple letter of perhaps six or eight lines written on high school notebook letter that read, "I have a question your book didn't answer for me. I believe in God and I believe in everything that you said, but I've always been taught that there is a Devil. Can you explain to me what that means?" Marianne wrote a two-page typewritten letter in answer. "That's the kind of attention and care Marianne pays," Harvey says.

What effect did *A Return to Love* have on the sales of the three-volume *A Course in Miracles*? The Foundation for Inner Peace, the course publishers, and the Foundation for *A Course in Miracles*, which prepares translations of the course, has had experience with another popularization of the course, Gerald Jampolski's *Love Is Letting Go of Fear*, which is based on some course principles. That book hit the best-seller lists a few years ago, but its impact on course sales was negligible. Keenly aware of the yawning gap between reading a book *on* the course and actually committing to studying the course itself, both Kenneth Wapnick and Bob Skutch are reticent to hazard an estimate on the ultimate effect *Return* will have on sales of *A Course in Miracles* and the number of its students. Skutch had expected HarperCollins to put the foundation's address in *Return to Love*, which they did as of the seventh printing. The *Course* itself has sold over 850,000 copies in hardcover and trade paper, he says, averaging 60,000 copies annually, "with no advertising." The *L.A. Reader* made a few inquiries when Marianne's book first hit the best-seller charts, and reported that *Course* sales had indeed been affected. According to Jane Ileil, director of trade and academic merchandising for Baker & Taylor, demand for *A Course in Miracles* jumped over five hundred percent since *Return* hit the marketplace. *A Return to Love* did "incredibly well," Nancy Oakley of Berkeley's Cody's Books told *Newsweek*. "It's almost become addictive for people," she says. "I would call it frenzied dependency."

* * *

In June of 1992, approximately one month before her fortieth birthday, Marianne stood before a packed auditorium of women, gathered for a lecture intensive. Dressed up for her sisters in a sleek-fitting fuchsia jacket with matching short pleated chiffon skirt and spike heels, she talked about her approaching milestone and reminded her audience that "we are ultimately responsible for the experience of our experience. I said to myself, 'Oh, I have this thing in front of me called the forties. Now what will my forties be like?' I realized that I'm not a passive observer to my life. Or if I choose to be a passive observer, I can be, and that's called misery," she quipped.

In her view, the course balances destiny and free will, Marianne explained, by teaching that "we are destined to have certain experiences in terms of their objective circumstances, but we are totally free to do what we will with those circumstances and experiences. So then I asked myself, 'What do I want my forties to be?' It made me recognize how different the deepest desires of my heart are from the dominant social stimulus of this world. As I started thinking about this, I realized the real shortcomings that exist in the major cultural stimulus. I realized for myself, as I'm sure you have for yourselves, that it goes much deeper than something men do to us. It's also what we do to ourselves. I found my womanhood would take as much work in the sense that I had to build, and continue to build, a context for that in my mind every bit as much as for my professional or any other endeavors."

It was clearly time for Marianne to rest and re-group, and perhaps to turn inward and nourish her feminine. Marianne had resigned from the Los Angeles Center for Living board, she had delivered her final regularly scheduled lecture, and her book was still solid on the best-seller nonfiction charts. But she continued to serve on the New York Center for Living's board and had donated her entire first royalty check to that charity.

Everywhere her visionary mind turned these days, new and urgent areas of need seemed to crop up. During the Los Angeles uprising, for example, Marianne called Sandy Scott, saying, "What can we do? What do you want to do?" The women met at Scott's house to pray and share ideas on how to help. Marianne called a press conference asking for a citywide Minute of Peace for Los Angeles. "Nothing stops her," Scott marvels. "She just wrote a huge check. She said, 'Well, I gave it because God told me to do that.' The reason I can't talk about it is that she's interested in doing anonymous things. She doesn't need her name on everything."

And here it was, one brief week after her "last" lecture, and Marianne was running a women's in-tensive, announcing her annual Fourth of July lec-ture a few weeks later, and a weekend seminar on relationships shortly after that.

In October 1991 Cynthia O'Neal founded her own AIDS charity, Friends in Deed, now located a few blocks from the New York Center for Living. Rather than viewing each other as rivals, as they have been characterized in the press, the two organizations regard each other as allies in the same cause, and sometimes coordinate their activities.

Marianne has characterized her experience as a lecturer as ninety percent joy, and her experience with the Centers for Living as ninety percent pain. Writing had delivered the greatest reward for her effort thus far, enabling her to communicate the course message to a far larger audience, with less chance of being the target of unwanted projections.

"I think one of the first things that hurt me most was some of the press calling me a guru," she says. "My own feeling is that is an area where I was always clear. When the press pictured me otherwise, I was hurt deeply because it is so untrue. Someone had said to me, 'Well, maybe I can get you on *Good Morning America,* and I said, 'No, I don't think I want anything like that right now.' Then, of course, promoting the Centers for Living became my job as president of the board, but I never told people at lectures, 'Come back, bring your friends'—nothing like that. Also, I'm Jewish; Jews don't proselytize. I'm skeptical, in the same way anybody is. You're always looking for those hooks. What do they really want? One of the things I learned from being a singer was to ask myself, 'Who am I trying to impress?' What I would answer is, 'If I walked into this club and I was sitting in the back seats, would I be impressed?' I wanted to be somebody I would like. I also wanted to be someone *I* would like when I lectured. I don't like anything where the hook finally comes. I knew that the people I would respect would always be looking for that hook, and that I would finally earn their respect. I was very naive," she admits, "and that has its up and its down sides."

In her "final" regularly scheduled lecture, Marianne discussed the issue of betrayal.

"Someone said hideous, hideous things about me in a magazine and in a newspaper—one of them actually used her name," Marianne began. "I made a joke to Richard [Cooper] afterward, 'I should have had lunch with her, Richard.' I thought to myself, 'How could this have happened? How could this woman have said these things about me? I know her!' I couldn't believe it. She wrote me a letter, and at the end she didn't apologize, but she wrote something like, 'Maybe if we had had lunch, I could have told you these things two years ago.'

"I realized that almost every person who had said horrible things about me had really wanted more attention," Marianne explained. "What they really wanted was more of my love. When they felt they weren't getting it, this is what happened. I also learned you can't withhold from your enemies, and say 'I'm not going to bless my enemies.' Jesus said, 'Bless your enemies, pray for your enemies.' He means so they won't be your enemies anymore. Having horrible things said about you in the press is a great lesson in forgiveness. You have to forgive them, because if you don't, they'll get you back in the next article. You have to try to neutralize it, so you start praying for your enemies big-time. Doesn't that make sense? You've got to send love in the direction where it hasn't been."

There were, of course, moments of unadulterated

oy. *A Return to Love* had its genesis on Valentine's Day, 1988, when Al Lowman suggested that Marianne write a book and offered to represent her. Four years later to the day, Marianne and Lowman were in Washington, D.C., for the first stop on her book tour, a Valentine's Day appearance on *Larry King Live.* "I woke up the next morning," recalls Lowman, "and I realized, not only was I still mateless, but here I was four years later in a Marianne Williamson framework. I sent flowers to her hotel room just down the hall, with a note that read, 'Happy Valentine's Day, which now means to me, Happy Anniversary. We'll always be bonded like this.' "

Two days before, on February 12, Norman Lear had thrown a party for Marianne to celebrate the publication of her book and launch her book tour. "What a nice thing that was," Lowman recalls. "First of all, the party occurred on the very day her book was announced as the number-one best-seller, which was unknown at the time the party was set up. Only she and I knew coming into the party. The books had just reached the stores when the show aired. By official publication date, there were 750,000 copies in print."

It was an intimate gathering for all of Marianne's friends, Lowman notes, not "a bullshit Hollywood party. I remember driving to the party with Marianne that night, and I felt like we were just floating down Sunset Boulevard."

Andrea Cagin says, when she arrived at the party, Marianne "rushed up to me and said, 'The book is number one, we did it! I'm gonna announce it.' We

just looked at each other like . . . 'Unbelievabl
What have we done?'"

Unfortunately, a crash back to earth was imm
nent. While in Philadelphia to promote her bool
Lowman handed Marianne a fax copy of the March
People magazine. Lowman says he'll never forget th
moment when he presented Marianne with the art
cle:

> I personally witnessed something so hor-
> rific; the absolute pain she expressed almost
> came from the bowels of the earth. There
> was a part of Robin's story that was savage. I
> don't think Marianne has ever had the expe-
> rience with the press that she had with this
> book. We really found out some things, even
> some eye-openers for me, and I think I'm re-
> ally savvy about the press. The only press
> that really upset her was the print media in
> New York and Los Angeles. Everything else
> was pretty much straight to the point, either
> about her work or her book or something
> having to do with her lifestyle, which is actu-
> ally modest and noneventful.

In a lecture on anger, Marianne talked about
"mind-boggling" phenomenon: "Two things bring u
darkness in people," she says, "your darkness ar
your light. Otherwise you would have to look :
Jesus and say, 'You know, he had a lot of negativi
in him to arouse all that stuff in people.' If you hav
negativity in you, people get crazy in your presenc

If you have light in you, people get crazy in your presence. For most of us, it's some of both that brings up people's craziness. When we can't let the light in, it's our projections. We get crazy in front of that and deny it every bit as much as we do in front of the negativity in people. I have felt in my career that people were more forgiving of my darkness than my light. In front of my darkness they tend to be compassionate; in front of my light, they're more inclined to go into attack and craziness. And yet," she continues, "that makes sense in *A Course in Miracles* terms because that's when ego will go crazy and those are our deepest teachings. To let in the light is more difficult for us than to let in the darkness."

Marianne once played with the notion of putting together a sort of stand-up/lecture show with Jungian interpreter and performer Pat Allen. The venture didn't work out, but they have remained good friends. "The Marianne Williamson I know is a very tender woman doing the best she can to carry God's message to as many people as she can and do as much good work as she can," Allen says. "I almost feel fear and trepidation about calling her to see how much damage is being created by this next level. It's like, 'Big sister, how's it going for you?' because my book comes out in January, and I'm facing the same kinds of issues. I, too, am not a killer woman. I really want to do my best. But it's not what your gift is, it's how it's marketed. It's what you're made to look like.

"I've cringed seriously at some of the statements I see written up in various tabloids about Marianne,"

Allen continues. "The Marianne I read about is not the Marianne I know over lunch. I don't know that mercenary thing, whatsoever. She approached me, saying, 'Pat, wouldn't it be fun if we could work a thing together?' It wasn't, 'Now, look here, we'll split the house . . .' It was, 'Let's get on the stage and see if we can do something together!' The truth is, we're too equal. We play to our audiences too much, and we've each got our schtick. Laurel and Hardy we are not. Our goal was that, and so it was painful when we bumped, but it was joyous too.

"I believe that there is a misconception that drab, dump, poor, and starving is the way you manifest God's message," Allen adds. " 'Dear God, I like Armani suits,' please! I like her willingness to have a child without a husband, her willingness to carry the message and to write a book that makes a difference in people's lives. I like the fact that she had a commercial past as a singer. I hate the thought that saints are born that way. I like the Augustinian route, that you go through life learning lessons, and you gradually distill your lessons until you want to carry your message to somebody else. That's the way I see it.

"I'm an old, recovering drunk," Allen says, "and so I came by somewhat the same route. I'm sure when I get my book out and it makes a dollar or two, somebody will discover I was a drunk at one time. Then they'll have to decide if my message isn't valid because I was a drunk, or whether I evolved through that process to a lesson where somebody else might be able to hear me better."

Marianne often speaks of Pollyanna, that cautionary object of ridicule amongst sophisticates, whose malignment parallels the contempt with which a message of unconditional love and positivity is sometimes regarded. "The story of Pollyanna is very interesting," she recently commented. "Pollyanna is a very powerful symbol. The ego knows this, which is why she's invalidated in this culture. It's ironic that when people want to insult you or in some way invalidate your spirituality, they say 'You're just being a Pollyanna.' If you read the story, though, you notice how powerful she was. She walks into a situation where everyone has been in total hell for years. The old lady's obnoxious and the old man's unhappy, and everybody is in this terrible dysfunction and unhappiness. She's there for what—two weeks? In the end, the entire situation has been turned around.

"She didn't go into denial and refuse to see the reality of the situation," Marianne explains. Pollyanna's consciousness was the space of creating a radical shift in circumstances. She didn't relate to the fear in people, she related to their love. She held her own mind open to the truth, and in her presence people could see the truth more clearly themselves. This is the gift of Jesus or any other enlightened master, because they see us in our true state. When we're around them we can see more clearly ourselves."

"Do I see signs of darkness all around me?" Marianne asked on another occasion. "Yes, when I choose to look at them. Do I see signs of hope and light all around me? Yes, I also see that. But I'm no interested in cursing the darkness. I'm interested in lighting a few candles."

Marianne Williamson herself has historically im pressed others as a Pollyanna, albeit one with per sonality. "Marianne is exactly the same to me," says writer Stanley Crouch today, a somewhat comica assessment considering the long and eventful jour ney she has taken since Crouch directed Marianne in his play at Pomona College. But then, again, the course's goal is to dismantle ego, not personality Crouch says:

> She's a strong-willed woman who wants things to be good and who has a vision of life based on a certain kind of sympathy. The weight of her own loneliness, her difficulties, her exasperations, and her disappointments are not going to change because she has a way to help people get out of a certain kind of emotional desolation. If Jesus woke up in the morning and was depressed, he'd be de pressed! Or Muhammed or Buddha, or any one else. You're not going to stop being human because you have the talent to do something people like.
>
> But Marianne is almost naive in her ex pectations, which leads to a certain exasper ation I don't think is based on a realistic way of looking at things. She has a grip on a pop ulist spirituality which fits in with the quick fix inclinations of our era. This may not be

what her intention is, but when you get into the spiritual show business, once you have a certain level of following, you are in show business. People come to see *you*. Even Moses found out he was in show business when he came back from Mount Sinai and they were dancing in the streets, having sex and bowing down before a golden calf. "Oh well, if not me, this!"

The inclination is toward show business/ entertainment as much as it is to any kind of deep feeling, besides the fact that America has enormous problems with the short, often brutal, and disappointing speed with which people reveal themselves to be less than you expect them to be . . .

Another reason why Marianne is success-ful is because even when she's trying to be honest in a way that reveals the culprits of the world, it has a cheerleaderlike innocence that I think is even more appealing than what she's saying. She doesn't have the slightest aspect of being jaded in her person-ality.

I was looking for a photograph taken of a scene in a three-woman show she was also in at Pomona, where Marianne was standing in front of two women, and all three were walking somewhere with a determined look on their faces. I'll never forget what Mari-anne said when she looked at it then. "This would be a perfect women's liberation photograph." I mentioned that to someone else at the time, and they said, "Of course, to her it would be that because the other two women are following her." Lo and behold, twenty years later, there you are!

Marianne Williamson is commited to her career as an author, but the publisher of her next book will be Random House, not HarperCollins.

Marianne was quoted as saying that her reasons for leaving HarperCollins were not financial and that the two offers were quite comparable. "There was an attitude at Random House that was very appealing to me," Ms. Williamson told *The Times*. "I felt very wanted."

Marianne's tour of this country to promote *A Return to Love* had also provided her with the opportunity to sense the collective mood of despair. After meditating on what she had observed, Marianne fixed on the subject of *The Healing of America*.

The theme concerns "reenvisioning this country," says Al Lowman, "how we can return to the original founding principles—at the time, radical spiritual concepts—such as 'in God we trust,' or 'E pluribus unum,' or any of the Jeffersonian doctrines that led to the Declaration of Independence and the Constitution. It's no longer someone else's disease or someone else's homelessness or someone else's violence or someone else's drug problem, or someone else's anything," he explains. "These problems touch all of us, and it is our collective responsiblity to clean it up. She feels too that the time is coming for a spiritual awakening in the country, which has made for Marianne Williamson's mainstream success. Marianne Williamson just happens to be a very gifted popularizer of people's innermost desires right now," Lowman says. "Labels that have sharply divided people, such as conservative, Democrat, blacks, whites, and so forth, are being thrown out the window. No one interest group, no one political party, can heal this country, as we used to think when we believed those problems were external." Based on her research into the founding fathers and mothers, whose philosophies are surprisingly compatible with that espoused by *A Course in Miracles*, Lowman continues, Marianne will set forth "some very pragmatic ways of reenvisioning this country on a subject by subject basis, such as motherhood and children, which is where she feels it really starts."

Marianne had already begun initial work on *Healing* with Andrea Cagin, when her own ongoing and relentless self-improvement process led to the notion of writing a book on women. She decided to tackle it first, in order to share what she has learned —particularly since she has become a mother—concerning the nature of the feminine. Marianne's universalizing of her personal issues could be misconstrued as egotistical, but, in fact, it proceeds from an opposite premise: the course teaching that despite the illusions of personality and body, we are all essentially the same.

"The people who've read the material I've written

so far have been surprised because it's a very men-friendly book," she says. "I'm glad that they felt that way because I think that the issues that confront us go much deeper than anything we can project and blame all on men.

"I feel very much a product of my parents, their weaknesses and their strengths," she said recently. "I'm just beginning at this point of my life to see where therapy and going back to the past fits in with *A Course in Miracles.*

"I go back into therapy at times because I recognize that I'm like a lot of women my age," she explained. "We became Amazons. The way we handle the fact that men hurt us is we don't let anybody hurt us again because we don't let them get close enough. I've realized that the only way I can allow myself to be more penetrable is by looking at some of that stuff—not to blame my parents, but to feel the pain and emote it.

"In the book I'm writing about women I talk about Scarlett O'Hara in *Gone with the Wind* saying, 'I'll never go hungry again.' It's like 'I'll never need a man again.'

"Pat [Allen] changed my life with men," Marianne says. "She says if at puberty your father respected your achievements more than he cherished your feelings, you become a woman who achieves in order to love. Then you find out achievement is not what makes love.

"I think that's exactly what women like us do," Marianne says, and then looks adoringly at her two-year-old daughter. "I give her so much space," she says. "I treat her like she's fifteen years old, for that very reason. People have told me they've never seen such an independent baby. They're supposed to go through a cuddly stage, and then become independent. She never went through the cuddly stage. She came out the womb basically ready to live. She's everything to me."

Is a political career in Marianne Williamson's future? "She has the force to be a political superstar," says Jaquel Prier. "She can help people with prayer and the *Course in Miracles* and turning it over to a higher power that can affect our entire political system. And that's not necessarily Democratic or Republican."

Judith Skutch, whose earlier career lecturing on *A Course in Miracles* is somewhat analogous to Marianne's, retired from the lecture circuit after an audience member kissed the hem of her skirt. "There may come a time in Marianne's life, in another phase, when she is in a quiet space," Skutch suggests. "Evelyn Underhill in her book *The Life of the Mystics,* written, I think, in 1928, made a very interesting observation, which I'll paraphrase. It didn't matter what mode of mysticism a person was practicing; when he or she received a revelation or studied something that was very real, he or she would go out into the world and share it. Sometimes it would be at the level of the masses, and sometimes just in a school setting. Then the need would come to go within, to integrate and come to yet another level.

That would be a time when a person could be a recluse. Then when that level was achieved, there would seem to be the impetus to go out and teach at that level, and again come back in for deepening.

"I think we're all doing that," Skutch says. "Eventually Marianne may feel a time when the public function for her is over. Remembering what I did when I was her age, and watching other people who performed a similar function, such as my friend Jerry Jampolski, who was very much in the public eye, there comes a time when everything you have taught yourself starts to take and you need to go to a quiet place for a while, maybe even for the rest of your life. For me, I think it's the rest of my life. There's something so glorious about that. It's nice when you look back and say, 'I've made some big mistakes here but they were all used.'"

Stanley Crouch says:

What is most interesting about Marianne at this point is what she will go on to become. I don't think she's going to become a hip version of Billy Graham. That's not going to happen to her.

Marianne is a very curious person who has a willingness to have adventures. She may set up a whole apparatus that may work with these people, but I think she will pursue something else. I don't see her staying in this arena, not because of boredom, but because I think there's a greater restlessness to her personality than people may be aware of at this point. She's looking for something, and she's been fortunate enough to ask questions about the nature of spiritual life that affirms something about our time of the machine age.

My feeling is that every generation must finally face the fact that the job is to sustain or extend civilization. I think Marianne has a feeling for that. Marianne's real aspiration to do something of value for civilization may carry her beyond what she is presently doing.

Norma Ferrara, known as Marianne's "California mother" and "the lady with the hat," has greeted Marianne's lecture audiences at the door since that first talk for the Philosophical Research Society. "I look upon her as my daughter," Ferrara says. "She is the most generous and giving person I've ever met; a lot of people have benefited from knowing Marianne. I wish for her what she's done for other people, that she finds peace and happiness in her life. I'm sure she will."

But no one knows Marianne Williamson's future, least of all herself. "I lecture on goals and vision," says Howard Rochestrie. "I've never, ever, met someone in my life who plays at her level who is not thinking, 'Okay, where do I want to be in two years, in five years.' I would ask her, 'What's your goal, what's your vision? Where do you want to be in three years, in five years?' And consistently she'd give me the same answer: 'Howard, you don't get it. What it's about is constantly asking the question, 'How can I serve? The answer is there.' "

Eternal Wisdom for Today's Lifestyles

LINDA GOODMAN'S STAR SIGNS

Linda Goodman is the most respected name in astrology and metaphysics. With her usual compassion, wit, and perception, she has now written the definitive guide to putting established knowledge to work for all her readers in today's fast-paced world. It will lead you to discover your latent powers, to control your personal destiny, and to recall the forgotten harmony of the Universe.

LINDA GOODMAN'S STAR SIGNS
_____ 95191-4 $6.99 U.S./$7.99 Can.